MEAT PIES & PUDDINGS

MEAT PIES & PUDDINGS

by Anne Chamberlain

LONDON
W FOULSHAM & CO LTD
New York Toronto Cape Town Sydney

W Foulsham & Co Ltd
Yeovil Road, Slough, Berks, England

ISBN 0-572-01039-7

Photoset and printed in Great Britain by
Lowe & Brydone Printers Limited, Thetford, Norfolk

CONTENTS

METRICATION

It is very important to use either the imperial table for measuring ingredients *or* the metric one, and not to mix them when preparing a recipe. The metric scale is not an exact translation of the imperial one, which would be very cumbersome, but the recipes have been tested to arrive at the correct proportions. The metric result is approximately 10% less than that gained with imperial measurements.

The metric scale recommended for British use allows 25 g to 1 oz; and 25 ml to 1 fl oz, instead of the true scale of 28 g to 1 oz. This means that quantities must be 'rounded up' at certain points on the scale, or else vital amounts will be lost as total recipe quantities become larger.

Solid Measures

½ oz	15 g
1 oz	25 g
2 oz	50 g
3 oz	75 g
4 oz	100 g
5 oz	125 g
6 oz	150 g
7 oz	175 g
8 oz	225 g
9 oz	250 g
10 oz	300 g
11 oz	325 g
12 oz	350 g
13 oz	375 g
14 oz	400 g
15 oz	425 g
16 oz	450 g or 500 g
1½ lb	750 g
2 lb	1 kg

Liquid Measures

½ fl oz	15 ml
1 fl oz	25 ml
2 fl oz	50 ml
3 fl oz	75 ml
4 fl oz	100 ml
¼ pint	125 ml
⅓ pint	175 ml
½ pint	250 ml
⅔ pint	350 ml
¾ pint	375 ml
1 pint	500 ml
1¼ pints	625 ml
1½ pints	750 ml
1¾—2 pints	1 litre

When meat and vegetables and some groceries are purchased in metric measure, they will normally be in 1 lb or 2 lb measurement equivalents, and people will ask for .5 kg or 1 kg which is 500 g or 1000 g. When baking, a measurement of 450 g is in proportion with the smaller amounts of ingredients needed.

INTRODUCTION

Savoury pies and puddings are deservedly popular because the pastry keeps all the rich juices inside the pie, and the result is a succulent filling contrasting with crisp pastry. Pastry originally formed a firm casing for food which might have to be carried a long way, and it is still handy for packed meals since it can taste just as good cold as hot. Not only does pastry enhance the chosen fillings, but it also serves as a useful extender so that a small quantity of expensive meat can be used for a number of portions. Start with the simple recipes in this book and then start to create your own delicious fillings according to the availability of ingredients – leftovers, for instance, can be quickly transformed into tasty supper flans. When you are making up a dish, be generous with pastry and use any leftover for some individual pies or a sweet dish, or for, perhaps, a few jam tarts for teatime.

While pastry-making can be fun, it can be time-consuming in a busy household, and there is no reason why frozen pastry or pastry mixes should not be used with the suggested fillings in this book. For this reason, the recipes give quantities of *made* pastry so that they can easily be used with home-made or commercially prepared pastry.

All recipes give 4—6 servings, according to appetite.

* = *Suitable for freezing*—**H or C** = *hot or cold*

Chapter One

ALL ABOUT PASTRY

Pastry-making is not difficult, but it is important to follow a few basic rules. Except for hot-water pastry, keep all ingredients cool and work in cool conditions. Use good fresh ingredients and weigh them carefully. Bake at the correct temperatures, and you should always find your pastry is tempting.

Ingredients

Use plain flour for the best results, and for puff pastry, use strong plain (bread) flour which helps to keep the lovely flaky layers in the pastry. Always use the proportion of fat to flour given in the recipe, as too little will make pastry hard, and too much will make it very 'short' and unmanageable. Equal quantities of margarine and lard make good pastry, and the fat should be just soft enough to rub in easily.

Methods

Fat should not be over-rubbed into the flour as this makes the pastry break when rolled out. The fat should be rubbed in lightly with fingers and thumbs until the mixture is like fine breadcrumbs. Very little water is necessary to mix the pastry – usually about 2 tablespoons chilled water to 8 oz/225 g/2 cups flour. This should be added all at once and the dough should be firm but not sticky.

Roll out the pastry on a cool surface, preferably on a marble slab or enamel table, and handle the pastry as little as possible. If the pastry is shaped into an approximate square, rectangle, circle or oval before rolling, it will save unnecessary handling.

Lift the pastry on the rolling pin to put it into a container, or over a filling, but do not stretch the pastry or it will shrink again during cooking. Re-roll trimmings to make decorations and attach them to the pie with a little water or beaten egg. Brush pastry with a little egg or milk to glaze it, and cut a small hole or slit in the lid to allow steam to escape.

Baking

Preheat the oven before putting in the pie, and if possible put a metal baking sheet on the oven shelf during this time. The pie can then be put on to this hot metal which will spread the heat evenly. Bake in the centre or at the top of the oven, and if the pastry browns too quickly, cover it with a piece of foil or greaseproof paper.

Baking Blind

A pastry case may be partly or completely baked before filling , and this is known as *baking blind*. Line the uncooked pastry case with foil or greaseproof paper and fill with baking beans, rice or crusts of bread so that the bottom does not rise during cooking. If preferred, prick the base with a fork and line with foil, but do not use beans, etc. Take this lining out about 5 minutes before the end of cooking, to allow the base to become firm.

Basic Recipes

The following recipes serve as guides to the ingredients and methods used for most pastry. To calculate the finished weight of pastry, add the total flour and fats and any other weighed ingredients, e.g., 8 oz/ 225 g/2 cups flour makes about 12 oz/350 g/¾ lb shortcrust pastry. If there is a little pastry left from a recipe, use it for some individual pies, cheese straws or tartlets.

Shortcrust Pastry

	Imperial	Metric	American
Plain flour	8 oz	225 g	2 cups
Salt	½ tsp	½ tsp	½ tsp
Margarine	2 oz	50 g	4 tbsp
Lard	2 oz	50 g	¼ cup
Cold water	2—3 tbsp	2—3 tbsp	2—3 tbsp

Sift together flour and salt. Rub in fat until mixture resembles fine breadcrumbs. Add water and mix to a stiff dough. Turn out on to a floured board and knead lightly until smooth. Roll out to required shape and thickness. Bake in a fairly hot oven, 425 °F/220 °C/Gas Mark 7 for 20—25 minutes.

Puff Pastry

	Imperial	Metric	American
Plain flour	1 lb	450 g	4 cups
Salt	1 tsp	1 tsp	1 tsp
Hard margarine	1 lb	450 g	2 cups
Lemon juice	2 tsp	2 tsp	2 tsp
Water (as cold as possible)	½ pint less 1 tbsp	250 ml less 1 tbsp	1¼ cups less 1 tbsp

Sift together flour and salt. Divide margarine into four. Rub one quarter into flour and then mix to a pliable dough with lemon juice and water. Turn out on to a floured board and knead well until smooth. Rest 15 minutes in a cool place. With 2 knives, form remaining margarine into a slab 5 in/12.5 cm square on a floured board. Roll dough into an oblong 11 x 6 in/27.5 x 15 cm. Place slab of fat on top end of dough, leaving a margin of about ½ in/1.25 cm along sides and top. Fold rest of dough over, placing upper edges of dough together. Brush off surplus flour.

First rolling   Turn pastry round so that folded edge is on left-hand side. Press three open edges together with rolling pin to seal. Press dough across about 5 times with rolling pin to flatten. Roll out into an oblong about 12 x 6 in/30 x 15 cm keeping edges straight.

Second rolling   Fold pastry in three by folding bottom third upwards and top third downwards and over to cover it. Turn so that folded edge is again on the left. Seal edges and roll out as before. Fold, turn and seal edges as before. Place pastry on floured plate in a polythene bag and rest in a cold place for 20 minutes.

Third to sixth rollings   Roll out 4 more times, always turning and sealing dough as before. Rest 20 minutes between each rolling. If any patches of fat still show, give dough another rolling. Rest dough before rolling out to ¼ in/6 mm or required thickness. Trim edges. Glaze with egg or milk before baking.

Rough Puff Pastry

	Imperial	Metric	American
Plain flour	8 oz	225 g	2 cups
Salt	½ tsp	½ tsp	½ tsp
Lard	3 oz	75 g	⅜ cup
Hard margarine	3 oz	75 g	⅜ cup
Water	6—8 tbsp	6—8 tbsp	6—8 tbsp

Sift flour and salt into a basin. Cut up fat roughly into small pieces, about ¼ in/6 mm cubes. Add to flour and mix to a soft dough with water. Roll out on a floured board to an oblong, approximately 6 x 12 in/15 x 30 cm and fold bottom third upwards and top third downwards and over it. Turn dough so that folded edge is on left-hand side and seal edges. Roll, fold and seal edges twice more, keeping folded edge always to the left. If pastry becomes too soft, chill between rollings. Roll out to required size, usually between ⅛—¼ in/3—6 mm thick. Trim edges. Glaze with egg or milk before baking.

Hot Watercrust Pastry

	Imperial	Metric	American
Plain flour	12 oz	350 g	3 cups
Salt	1 tsp	1 tsp	1 tsp
Lard	5 oz	150 g	5/8 cup
Milk and water mixed	1/4 pint	125 ml	1/2 cup

Sift flour and salt into a warm bowl. Put lard, milk and water into a pan, heat until fat melts, then bring to the boil. Pour at once into the centre of flour, and, using a wooden spoon, form into a paste. Turn out on to a lightly floured board and knead quickly till smooth. Hot watercrust pastry must be used while warm; it becomes stiff and unmanageable as it gets cooler. To keep warm, cover and stand in a warm place.

To mould: cut off one-third of pastry for lip and decorations and keep warm. Roll out remaining pastry into a 10 in/25 cm circle, and line 6 in/15 cm greased cake tin with a removable base. Mould pastry from base and up sides until it is of even thickness, free from cracks and 1/4 in/6 mm higher than top of tin. Add meat filling. Roll out reserved pastry for a lid. Moisten edges with cold water. Cover pie with lid, press edges well together to seal, knock up and decorate.

If a loose-based cake tin is not available, mould rolled-out pastry over base of a 6 in/15 cm diameter greased jar, or other container, to come about 3½ in/9 cm up sides of jar. Place on baking sheet; then remove jar. Add filling and cover with lid as above.

Bake in centre of hot oven, 425 °F/225 °C/Gas Mark 7 for 30 minutes and then at 325—350 °F/170—180 °C/Gas Mark 3—4 for 1½ hours according to recipe. After 1½ hours cooking, brush top with beaten egg. Cover with paper during last stages of cooking if becoming too brown.

Chapter Two

SINGLE CRUST DEEP PIES

Shortcrust and puff pastry are both suitable for savoury pies made in deep earthenware pie dishes. The meat filling may be extended with vegetables, mushrooms, hard-boiled eggs and a savoury sauce or gravy, and the filling is usually cooked before the pastry is put on and finished in the oven. To save washing-up, it is sensible to cook the filling in the pie dish with a foil covering, and to cool it slightly before topping with pastry and finishing baking. Since the oven will be on for some time if this method is used, it is a good idea to cook some puddings or bake some cakes at the same time; fill up the odd spaces in the oven with baked potatoes to go with the pie, and some baked apples or other fruit which may be used as a pudding or as a breakfast dish. If a deep single-crust pie is to be frozen, it should be prepared with cooked filling and then topped with pastry. This may be cooked or left uncooked before freezing. It is easiest to make pies for the freezer in foil dishes so that a china or ovenglass dish is not out of use for some time.

Steak and Kidney Pie

*H	Imperial	Metric	American
Puff pastry	8 oz	225 g	½ lb
Plain flour	1 oz	25 g	¼ cup
Salt and pepper			
Stewing steak	1½ lb	750 g	1½ lb
Ox kidney	8 oz	225 g	½ lb
Lard	1 oz	25 g	2 tbsp
Medium onion	1	1	1
Button mushrooms	4 oz	100 g	1 cup
Stock	½ pint	250 ml	1¼ cups
Beaten egg	1	1	1

Put flour and plenty of seasoning in a polythene bag. Add cubed steak and kidney and shake the bag until the meat is coated with flour. Reserve any flour in the bag, and remove the meat. Melt lard and fry chopped onion until just tender but not brown. Add meat and brown quickly on all sides. Add halved mushrooms and cook for a minute. Stir in reserved flour, if any, and then add stock. Bring to the boil, cover and simmer gently for 1½—2 hours or until meat is tender. Put meat and mushrooms into a deep pie dish, with enough gravy to come halfway up the dish.

Roll out pastry to about 1 in/2.5 cm larger than the top of the pie dish. Cut out a long strip of pastry about ½ in/1.25 cm wide to fit the rim of the dish, and a pastry 'lid'. Moisten the rim of the dish, and press on the pastry strip. Moisten pastry strip and place 'lid' on dish. Press down well, to seal edges, trim off excess pastry, then knock edges together and flute with a knife.

Re-roll trimmings and cut out pastry leaves to decorate pie. Brush with beaten egg, place dish on a baking tray and bake at 425 °F/220 °C/Gas Mark 7 for 20 minutes. Reduce heat to 350 °F/180 °C/Gas Mark 4 and cook for a further 15 minutes.

Steak and Mushroom Pie

*H	Imperial	Metric	American
Puff pastry	8 oz	225 g	½ lb
Stewing beef	1 lb	500 g	1 lb
Madeira	3 tbsp	3 tbsp	3 tbsp
Button mushrooms	4 oz	100 g	1 cup
Shallots	8 oz	225 g	½ lb
Stock	4 tbsp	4 tbsp	4 tbsp
Salt and pepper			
Beaten egg	1	1	1

Cut the steak in cubes and leave to stand in the wine while the pastry is being made. Brown the meat in a little fat; then turn it into a pie dish, along with the other ingredients. Cover with a piece of foil and cook at 350 °F/180 °C/Gas Mark 4 for approximately 1¼ hours or until tender. Remove, uncover and cool.

Roll out the pastry to a rectangle slightly larger than the dish. Place the pastry on top of the pie dish, trim the edges and then flute with a knife. The trimmings may be used to decorate the top of the pie with pastry leaves. Brush the top of the pie with beaten egg and bake at 425 °F/220 °C/Gas Mark 7 for about 20 minutes or until well browned.

Steak and Ale Pie

*H	Imperial	Metric	American
Puff pastry	8 oz	225 g	½ lb
Lard	1 oz	25 g	2 tbsp
Chuck steak	1½ lb	750 g	1½ lb
Onion	1	1	1
Sticks of celery	4	4	4
Stock	¾ pint	375 ml	1⅞ cups
Salt and pepper			
Plain flour	1 oz	25 g	¼ cup
Beaten egg	1	1	1
Brown ale	½ pint	250 ml	1¼ cup

Cut the steak into 1½ in/3.75 cm cubes. Slice the onion and chop the celery. Melt lard and fry steak, onion and celery. Stir in stock and seasoning. Bring to the boil, cover and simmer for about 1½ hours until meat is tender. Mix flour with a little water to form a smooth paste. Stir into pan gradually. Bring to the boil, stirring. Turn meat and vegetables with half the gravy into a 1½ pint/750 ml/3¾ cup pie dish and cool. Roll out pastry and use to cover the pie. Brush with beaten egg. Bake at 425 °F/220 °C/Gas Mark 7 for 10 minutes. Reduce heat to 375 °F/190 °C/Gas Mark 5 for a further 20 minutes. Place ale in saucepan, and boil rapidly until reduced to ¼ pint/125 ml/⅝ cup. Before serving the pie, remove the crust and cut into triangular portions. Stir hot ale into meat and vegetables, and replace pastry crust.

Beef and Beer Pie

	Imperial	Metric	American
*H			
Puff pastry	12 oz	350 g	3/4 lb
Oil	2 tbsp	2tbsp	2tbsp
Large onions	2	2	2
Stewing beef	1 lb	500 g	1 lb
Ox kidney	8 oz	225 g	1/2 lb
Plain flour	1 1/2 oz	40 g	1/8 cup+ 2 tbsp
Salt and pepper			
Brown ale	1/2 pint	250 ml	1 1/4 cups
Water	1/4 pint	125 ml	5/8 cup
Thyme	1/4 tsp	1/4 tsp	1/4 tsp
Thinly peeled rind of orange	1/2	1/2	1/2
Worcestershire sauce	2 tbsp	2 tbsp	2 tbsp
Milk or beaten egg			

Heat oil in a large pan and fry chopped onions for 5 minutes. Cut beef and kidney into 1 in/2.5 cm cubes and toss in flour, seasoned with salt and pepper. Add to pan and cook for about 5 minutes more, stirring frequently until meat is browned. Remove from heat and gradually stir in ale and water.

Return to heat and bring to the boil, stirring all the time. Add thyme and orange rind. Cover pan and simmer for 1 1/2—2 hours until meat is tender. Remove orange rind, stir in Worcestershire sauce and allow to cool. Turn into a 2 pint/1 litre/5 cup pie dish.

Roll out the pastry and use to cover the pie dish. Trim and flute the edges. Brush the top of the pie with milk or beaten egg. Bake at 425 °F/220 °C/Gas Mark 7 for 25 minutes until pastry is golden brown.

Steak and Ham Pie

* H	Imperial	Metric	American
Puff pastry	8 oz	225 g	½ lb
Chuck steak	1 lb	450 g	1 lb
Uncooked ham	8 oz	225 g	½ lb
Pinch of thyme			
Pinch of parsley			
Pinch of ground nutmeg			
Salt and pepper			
Beef stock	¾ pint	375 ml	1⅞ cups
Egg yolk	1	1	1

Cut the beef and ham into small cubes and arrange in a pie dish. Sprinkle thickly with chopped thyme and parsley, nutmeg, salt and pepper. Pour on the stock. Cover with a lid or foil and cook at 350 °F/180 °C/Gas Mark 4 for 1 hour. Remove the lid, and cover the meat with pastry. Brush the surface with beaten egg yolk, and continue baking for about 1 hour until the pastry is golden.

Beef and Potato Pie

H	Imperial	Metric	American
Shortcrust pastry	8 oz	225 g	½ lb
Stewing steak	1 lb	450 g	1 lb
Onions	4 oz	100 g	¼ lb
Potatoes	1 lb	450 g	1 lb
Salt and pepper			
Water	¾ pint	375 ml	1⅞ cups

Cut the steak into cubes. Peel the onions and potatoes and slice them thinly. Arrange layers of meat, onions and potatoes in a pie dish, seasoning well with salt and pepper. Pour in the water. Cover with a piece of foil and cook at 375 °F/190 °C/Gas Mark 5 for 1½ hours. Remove the foil and cover the dish with pastry. Bake at 400 °F/200 °C/Gas Mark 6 for 25 minutes.

Lamb and Mushroom Pie

*H	Imperial	Metric	American
Shortcrust pastry	8 oz	225 g	½ lb
Shoulder lamb	1 lb	450 g	1 lb
Lambs' kidneys	2	2	2
Seasoned flour	1 tbsp	1 tbsp	1 tbsp
Lard	1 oz	25 g	2 tbsp
Medium onion	1	1	1
Stock	½ pint	250 ml	1¼ cups
Mushrooms	4 oz	100 g	¼ lb
Salt and pepper			
Beaten egg to glaze			

Cut the meat into cubes and chop the kidneys finely. Toss in the seasoned flour. Melt the lard and cook the chopped onion until golden. Stir in the lamb and kidney pieces and cook until lightly browned. Stir in the stock and halved mushrooms. Bring to the boil and then simmer until the meat is tender. Season with salt and pepper and turn into a pie dish. Cover with the pastry and brush with beaten egg to glaze. Bake at 400 °F/200 °C/Gas Mark 6 for 30 minutes.

Victorian Lamb Pie

*H	Imperial	Metric	American
Shortcrust pastry	12 oz	350 g	¾ lb
Lamb cut from leg	2 lb	1kg	2 lb
Lamb kidneys	2	2	2
Salt and pepper			
Parsley and thyme stuffing	6 oz	150 g	⅓ lb
Brown gravy	½ pint	250 ml	1¼ cups

Cut the lamb into thin slices, and cut the kidneys into pieces. Arrange half the lamb in the bottom of a pie dish and season with salt and pepper. Put on a layer of stuffing, and cover with the remaining lamb and kidney pieces. Pour on the gravy. Cover with pastry and bake at 375 °F/190 °C/Gas Mark 5 for 1¼ hours, covering the pastry with a piece of foil if it browns too quickly.

Gillyburn Chicken Pie

*H	Imperial	Metric	American
Shortcrust pastry	12 oz	350 g	¾ lb
Pork or beef sausages	8 oz	225 g	½ lb
Large pinch of mixed herbs			
Butter	1 oz	25 g	2 tbsp
Cooked chicken	12 oz	350 g	¾ lb
Flour	1 oz	25 g	¼ cup
Chicken stock	½ pint	250 ml	1¼ cups
Salt and pepper			
Beaten egg to glaze			

Skin the sausages, mix with the herbs, and shape into eight balls with floured hands. Heat ½ oz/15 g/1 tbsp butter in a frying pan and fry the sausages until golden brown. Place in a pie dish with the chopped chicken. Pour off half the fat, add the remaining butter and stir in the flour. Blend in the stock and bring to the boil, stirring well and season to taste. Pour into the pie dish and allow to cool. Roll out the pastry and cover the pie dish. Brush with beaten egg, make a hole in the centre and bake at 375 °F/190 °C/Gas Mark 5 for 30 minutes.

Pork and Kidney Pie

*H	Imperial	Metric	American
Shortcrust pastry	8 oz	225 g	½ lb
Pork shoulder	1 lb	450 g	1 lb
Pigs' kidneys	3	3	3
Mixed herbs	2 tsp	2 tsp	2 tsp
Stock	½ pint	250 ml	1¼ cups
Pinch of ground nutmeg			
Medium onion	1	1	1
Medium carrots	2	2	2

Chop the pork and kidneys into small pieces and put into a pie dish with the herbs, stock, nutmeg and finely chopped onion and carrots. Cover with a piece of foil and cook at 325 °F/170 °C/Gas Mark 3 for 1 hour. Remove the foil and cover the dish with a pastry lid. Bake at 400 °F/200 °C/Gas Mark 6 for 30 minutes.

Chicken and Leek Pie

	Imperial	Metric	American
H			
Puff pastry	12 oz	350 g	¾ lb
Chicken	3 lb	1.5 kg	3 lb
Cold water	3 pints	1.5 litre	7½ cups
Large onion	1	1	1
Bay leaves	2	2	2
Few parsley stalks			
Salt and pepper			
Medium leeks	6	6	6
Cooked ox tongue	4 oz	100 g	¼ lb
Beaten egg	1	1	1
Double cream	3 tbsp	3 tbsp	3 tbsp

Place chicken, water, onion, bay leaves and parsley stalks in a large saucepan. Season well, and bring to the boil. Cover and simmer gently for about 1¼ hours or until chicken is tender. Transfer chicken to a plate and allow to cool slightly. Reserve stock. Trim leeks to within 1 in/2.5 cm of the green stems, then wash well. Slice thinly, and place in a saucepan with about ¾ pint/375 ml/1⅞ cups chicken stock. Bring to the boil, cover and simmer gently for about 15 minutes, or until leeks are tender. Remove skin from chicken, then cut meat away from the bones. Discard skin and bones, and cut meat into 1 in/2.5 cm pieces. Arrange chicken in the bottom of a 2½—3 pint/ 1—1.5 litre/7 cup pie dish and place a pie funnel in the centre. Drain leeks, reserving stock, and arrange leeks over chicken. Pour ½ pint/150 ml/1¼ cups reserved stock into a dish. Cut sliced tongue into 1 in/2.5 cm strips, and arrange over leeks.

Roll out pastry to an oval approximately 2 in/5 cm larger than the pie dish. Cut out a lid for the dish, and a strip to fit rim of dish. Moisten rim of dish and press on pastry strip. Moisten pastry strip and place lid on pie. Seal edges well, then trim off excess pastry. Knock edges together and pinch decoratively. Use pastry trimmings to make leaves or a tassel, and arrange around centre of pie. Make a small hole in the centre of the pie. Brush pastry with beaten egg, and bake at 400 °F/200 °C/Gas Mark 6 for 40 minutes, until pastry is well risen and golden brown. Just before serving, warm cream in a saucepan, make a small funnel from aluminium foil, and pour cream into the pie through the hole in the centre of the pastry.

Chicken and Mushroom Pie

H	Imperial	Metric	American
Puff pastry	12 oz	350 g	¾ lb
White sauce	1 pint	500 ml	2½ cups
Cooked chicken	6 oz	150 g	⅓ lb
Mushrooms	4 oz	100 g	¼ lb
Salt and pepper			
Beaten egg to glaze			

Chop the chicken and slice the mushrooms. Combine all the filling ingredients, season to taste and turn into a 1½ pint/750 ml/3¾ cup oval pie dish.

Roll out pastry to just under ¼ in/6 mm thickness. Cut out lid to fit top of pie dish. Line edges of pie dish with strips of pastry. Moisten with water, cover with lid then press well together to seal. Flute the edges. Brush all over with beaten egg and decorate with leaves, rolled and cut out from trimmings. Bake towards top of oven at 450 °F/ 230 °C/Gas Mark 8 for 15 minutes then at 375 °F/190 °C/Gas Mark 5 for a further 15—20 minutes.

Chicken & Ox Tongue Pie

*H	Imperial	Metric	American
Puff pastry	12 oz	350 g	¾ lb
Chicken	3 lb	1.5 kg	3 lb
Cold water	3 pints	1.75 litre	7½ cups
Large onion	1	1	1
Bay leaves	2	2	2
Few parsley stalks			
Salt and pepper			
Courgettes	1 lb	450 g	1 lb
Cooked ox tongue	4 oz	100 g	¼ lb
Beaten egg to glaze			

Place chicken, water, onion, bay leaves and parsley in a large saucepan. Season well, and bring to the boil. Cover and simmer gently for about 1¼ hours, or until chicken is tender. Transfer chicken to a plate and allow to cool slightly. Reserve stock, removing bay leaves. Slice courgettes thinly, and place in a saucepan with about ¾ pint/375 ml/1⅞ cup reserved chicken stock. Bring to the boil, cover and simmer gently for about 15 minutes or until courgettes are tender. Skin chicken, then cut meat away from the bones and cut meat into 1 in/2.5 cm pieces. Arrange chicken in the bottom of a 2½—3 pint/1.5 litre/7 cup pie dish. Drain courgettes, reserving stock, and arrange them over chicken. Pour ½ pint/250 ml/1¼ cups reserved stock into a dish. Cut sliced tongue into 1 in/2.5 cm strips, and arrange over courgettes.

Roll out pastry to an oval, approximately 2 in/5 cm larger than the pie dish. Cut out a lid for the dish, and a strip to fit rim of dish. Moisten rim of dish and press on pastry strip. Moisten pastry strip and place lid on pie. Seal edges well, then trim off excess pastry. Knock edges together and pinch decoratively. Use pastry trimmings to make leaves or a tassel, and arrange around centre of pie.

Make a small hole in the centre of the pie. Brush pastry with beaten egg, and bake at 400 °F/200 °C/Gas Mark 6 for 30—40 minutes, or until pastry is well risen and golden brown.

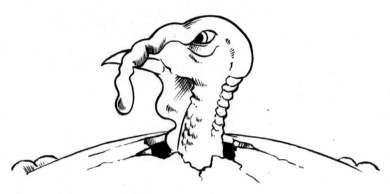

Turkey Pie

* H	Imperial	Metric	American
Puff pastry	12 oz	350 g	¾ lb
Cooked turkey	12 oz	350 g	¾ lb
Hard-boiled eggs	2	2	2
Butter	1 oz	25 g	2 tbsp
Plain flour	1 oz	25 g	¼ cup
Milk	¼ pint	125 ml	⅝ cup
Turkey stock	¼ pint	125 ml	⅝ cup
Juice and grated rind of lemon	½	½	½
Beaten egg	1	1	1
Salt and pepper			

Place the diced turkey and quartered hard-boiled eggs in a pie dish. Make a sauce with the butter, flour, milk and stock; bring to the boil, stirring well. Add lemon rind and juice and season well. Pour over the turkey. Roll out the pastry and cover the pie dish. Brush with the beaten egg, make a hole in the centre and bake at 425 °F/220 °C/ Gas Mark 7 for 30 minutes.

Chicken and Potato Pie

H	Imperial	Metric	American
Puff pastry	12 oz	350 g	¾ lb
Cooked chicken	1 lb	450 g	1 lb
Potatoes	1 lb	450 g	1 lb
Chicken stock	½ pint	250 ml	1¼ cups
Evaporated milk	½ pint	250 ml	1¼ cups
Chopped parsley	1 tbsp	1 tbsp	1 tbsp
Salt and pepper			

Cut the chicken and the peeled potatoes into small cubes. Make a rich chicken stock by simmering the carcass in water with plenty of herbs. Mix the stock and the evaporated milk and pour over the chicken and potato in a pie dish. Season well with salt and pepper, and stir in the parsley. Cover with pastry and bake at 425 °F/220 °C/Gas Mark 7 for 40 minutes.

Country Rabbit Pie

* H	Imperial	Metric	American
Shortcrust pastry	12 oz	350 g	¾ lb
Large rabbit	1	1	1
Sprig of parsley	1	1	1
Small onion	1	1	1
Fat bacon	12 oz	350 g	¾ lb
Stock	¼ pint	125 ml	⅝ cup
Salt and pepper			
Plain flour			

Joint the rabbit and leave it to soak in cold salted water for 6 hours. Drain the joints and wipe dry. Season with salt and pepper, chopped parsley and finely chopped onion. Cut the bacon into small pieces and put in the pie dish with the rabbit and a light sprinkling of flour. Pour in the stock. Cover with pastry and bake at 375 °F/190 °C/ Gas Mark 5 for 1¼ hours, covering the pastry with a piece of foil if it browns too quickly.

Rabbit and Steak Pie

*H	Imperial	Metric	American
Puff pastry	12 oz	350 g	¾ lb
Large rabbit	1	1	1
Stewing steak	8 oz	225 g	½ lb
Pork sausage meat	4 oz	100 g	¼ lb
Stock	½ pint	250 ml	1¼ cups
Salt and pepper			
Pinch of ground nutmeg			
Chopped parsley			

Joint the rabbit, soak in cold salted water, drain and dry. Cut the steak into cubes and make the sausage meat into small round balls. Arrange layers of rabbit, steak and sausage meat balls in a pie dish, seasoning well with salt, pepper, nutmeg and parsley. Add the stock and cover with pastry. Bake at 450 °F/230 °C/Gas Mark 8 for 15 minutes, and then at 350 °F/180 °C/Gas Mark 4 for 1 hour, covering the pastry if it browns too quickly.

Party Chicken Pie

H	Imperial	Metric	American
Puff pastry	8 oz	225 g	½ lb
Butter	3 oz	75 g	⅜ cup
Plain flour	3 oz	75 g	¾ cup
Chicken stock	1 pint	500 ml	2½ cups
Milk	¼ pint	125 ml	⅝ cup
Cooked chicken	12 oz	350 g	¾ lb
Mushrooms	8 oz	225 g	½ lb
Sticks of celery	2	2	2
Toasted blanched almonds	2 oz	50 g	2 heaped tbsp
Sherry or lemon juice	3 tbsp	3 tbsp	3 tbsp
Salt and pepper			
Pinch of ground nutmeg			
Beaten egg to glaze			

Roll out pastry into a 7 in/17.5 cm round or large enough to fit top of casserole dish. Trim edges and place on baking tray. Cut into six triangles, brush with beaten egg and decorate each piece with a pastry leaf, rolled and cut from trimmings. Leave pastry in a cool place to rest and prepare filling.

Melt butter in a pan, add flour and stir over a low heat for 2 minutes. Gradually stir in chicken stock and milk; then cook, stirring, until sauce comes to the boil and thickens. Add chopped chicken, sliced mushrooms, chopped celery, almonds, sherry or lemon juice and salt, pepper and nutmeg. Cover pan and cook mixture very gently for 15 minutes. Bake pastry towards top of a hot oven at 450 °F/230 °C/Gas Mark 8 for 10—12 minutes. Turn hot chicken mixture into a warmed casserole dish and arrange hot pastry triangles on top to serve.

Pigeon Pie

*H	Imperial	Metric	American
Shortcrust pastry	8 oz	225 g	½ lb
Streaky bacon	6 rashers	6 rashers	6 rashers
Medium onions	2	2	2
Pigeons	2	2	2
Hard-boiled egg yolks	2	2	2
Salt and pepper			
Chopped fresh parsley	1 tbsp.	1 tbsp	1 tbsp
Chicken stock	¼ pint	125 ml	⅝ cup
Water to mix			
Beaten egg to glaze			

The pigeons should be plucked, drawn and cut into four pieces. Line a 1½ pint/750 ml/3¾ cup pie dish with the bacon rashers. Sprinkle chopped onion over the top. Place pie funnel in centre and arrange pigeon pieces and halved egg yolks around it. Add seasoning, parsley and stock. Roll out pastry and use to cover pie, cutting out a hole over the funnel. Decorate with leaves made from pastry trimmings. Brush with beaten egg and bake at 350 °F/180 °C/Gas Mark 4 for 1½ hours. Lightly cover pastry lid with aluminium foil when golden brown in colour to prevent pastry overbrowning.

Country Winter Pie

H	Imperial	Metric	American
Shortcrust pastry	12 oz	350 g	¾ lb
White sauce	½ pint	250 ml	1¼ cups
Butter or margarine	2 oz	50 g	¼ cup
Leeks	8 oz	225 g	½ lb
Carrots	8 oz	225 g	½ lb
Celery	8 oz	225 g	½ lb
Parsnips	8 oz	225 g	½ lb
Cooked bacon or ham	8 oz	225 g	½ lb
Salt and pepper			

Melt 2 oz/50 g/¼ cup butter in a pan, add chopped or sliced vegetables and fry gently for 5 minutes. Add ¼ pint/125 ml/⅝ cup water and a little salt and simmer vegetables for 20 minutes; then drain. Combine with white sauce and chopped bacon or ham. Season to taste. Place in a 2 pint/1 litre/5 cup pie dish. Leave to cool.

Roll out pastry and cover top of pie. Flute the edges. Decorate top with leaves cut from pastry trimmings and make a hole in the centre. Glaze with a little milk or beaten egg. Bake at 400 °F/200 °C/Gas Mark 6 for 25—30 minutes.

Fidget Pie

H	Imperial	Metric	American
Shortcrust pastry	8 oz	225 g	½ lb
Lean back bacon	12 oz	350 g	¾ lb
Potatoes	1 lb	450 g	1 lb
Cooking apples	1 lb	450 g	1 lb
Salt and pepper			
Chicken stock	¼ pint	125 ml	⅝ cup
Beaten egg to glaze			

Cut each bacon rasher into three pieces. Arrange layers of sliced potatoes, bacon and sliced apples in a 2½—3 pint/1.5 litre/6—7 cup pie dish, until all ingredients are used, seasoning well between each layer. Pour chicken stock into the pie dish.

Roll out the pastry to an oval, approximately 2 in/5 cm larger than the pie dish. Cut out a 'lid' to fit the dish, and a strip of pastry about 1 in/2.5 cm wide to fit rim of the dish. Moisten rim of dish, and press on pastry strip. Moisten the pastry strip, and place the 'lid' on the dish. Seal edges well, then trim off excess pastry. Knock edges together, then pinch decoratively. Use trimmings to make pastry leaves, if liked. Brush with beaten egg and bake towards the bottom of the oven at 400 °F/200 °C/Gas Mark 6 for 20 minutes, then reduce to 350 °F/180 °C/Gas Mark 4 and continue to cook for 45 minutes.

Harvest Pie

H	Imperial	Metric	American
Shortcrust pastry	12 oz	350 g	¾ lb
Boiled bacon	1 lb	450 g	1 lb
Butter	1 oz	25 g	2 tbsp
Flour	1 oz	25 g	¼ cup
Bacon stock	¼ pint	125 ml	½ cup
Milk	¼ pint	125 ml	½ cup
Chopped hard-boiled eggs	2	2	2
Small onion	1	1	1
Cooked peas	4 oz	100 g	¼ lb
Cooked carrots	6 oz	150 g	⅓ lb
Salt and pepper			

Remove skin and excess fat from bacon and cut into large cubes. Melt butter in a pan, add flour and cook for one minute, without browning. Remove from heat and gradually add bacon stock and milk. (If bacon stock is too salty use ½ pint/250 ml/1¼ cups milk.) Return to heat and bring to the boil to thicken, stirring all the time. Remove from heat and add remaining ingredients. Turn into a 2 pint/1 litre/5 cup pie dish and leave to cool. Roll out pastry ¼ in/6 mm thick and cover pie dish. Use trimmings to decorate. Bake at 425 °F/220 °C/Gas Mark 7 for 30 minutes.

Chapter Three

PLATE PIES AND SAVOURY ROLLS

Plate pies are useful both hot and cold, and slices of them will even serve for a packed meal. These pies with a top and bottom crust may be made in china flan dishes, sponge sandwich tins or flat metal or ovenglass plates. For freezing, they are best made in foil plates in which they can be frozen and reheated if necessary. Sometimes, the bottom crust of savoury pies become soggy, but if the pastry is brushed with a little melted lard and left until set before the filling is put in, the bottom pastry will remain crisp. A metal container is also much better at conducting heat than a china one and crisper pastry will be the result. It is also a good idea to put a metal baking sheet on the oven shelf while the oven is heating, and the plate pie can then be put on to this hot surface which will also help to make the pastry cook better and be crisper.

A slightly old-fashioned way of preparing pies is to enclose the filling in a single sheet of pastry, so that a savoury roll is formed which can be conveniently cut in slices. This is a delicious way of making a 'pie' and is very welcome to those who do not like too much pastry in their portions. Shortcrust or puff pastry may be used for savoury rolls and plaits.

Steak and Kidney Plate Pie

*H or C	Imperial	Metric	American
Puff pastry	12 oz	350 g	¾ lb
Stewing steak	1 lb	450 g	1 lb
Ox kidney	4 oz	100 g	¼ lb
Plain flour	1 tbsp	1 tbsp	1 tbsp
Salt and pepper			
Fat	1 oz	25 g	2 tbsp
Small onion	1	1	1
Water	½ pint	250 ml	1¼ cups
Mustard (prepared)	1 tsp	1 tsp	1 tsp
Beaten egg to glaze			

Cut the steak and kidney into small pieces and toss in flour seasoned with salt and pepper. Heat the fat and lightly brown the sliced onion. Add the meat and brown it lightly. Add the water, cover and simmer very gently for 1½ hours. Stir in the mustard.

Roll out the pastry and cut a strip to put round the edge of a moistened 9 in/22.5 cm pie plate. Moisten the top of the pastry strip. Turn the meat filling into the plate and put on a pastry lid. Press on to the pastry strip and decorate the edges. Slit the centre and brush the top with a little beaten egg or milk. Bake at 450 °F/220 °C/Gas Mark 8 for 15 minutes, and then at 375 °F/190 °C/Gas Mark 5 for 15 minutes.

Savoury Beef Roll

*H or C	Imperial	Metric	American
Shortcrust pastry	8 oz	225 g	½ lb
Raw minced beef	1 lb	450 g	1 lb
Breadcrumbs	3 oz	75 g	¾ cup
Small egg	1	1	1
Onion	1	1	1
Ground ginger	¼ tsp	¼ tsp	¼ tsp
Mixed herbs	½ tsp	½ tsp	½ tsp
Salt and pepper			
Beaten egg to glaze			

Put minced beef into a basin, add breadcrumbs, very finely chopped onion, herbs and spice. Mix thoroughly with the hand, then form into roll. Place in a well-greased tin, cover well with greased paper and bake at 375 °F/190 °C/Gas Mark 5 for 20 minutes.

Put pastry on a floured board and roll into an oblong. Remove the roll from the oven and taking off paper, wrap it quickly in the pastry. Put a few pastry leaves on top, brush over with milk or beaten egg, and return to oven. Cook for 30 minutes longer until the pastry is brown and thoroughly cooked. Serve with brown or tomato sauce.

Minced Beef Pie

*H or C

	Imperial	Metric	American
Shortcrust pastry	12 oz	350 g	3/4 lb
Minced fresh beef	12 oz	350 g	3/4 lb
Large onion	1	1	1
Carrot	1	1	1
Salt and pepper			
Parsley, thyme and bay leaf			
Thick gravy	1/2 pint	250 ml	1 1/4 cups

Place the meat, chopped onion, grated carrot, seasoning and herbs in a saucepan and bring to the boil. Add the gravy and leave to simmer gently for one hour. Line a 7 in/17.5 cm flan ring with half the pastry. Remove the herbs and pour meat mixture into the pastry case. If the gravy requires more thickening, blend in 1 tbsp cornflour mixed with a little water.

Cut remaining pastry into circles 1/4 in/6 mm thick and place on a separate baking sheet. Cover pie with foil and bake both pie and circles at 375 °F/190 °C/Gas Mark 5 for 30 minutes. Arrange pastry circles round top of pie before serving.

Corned Beef Pie

*H or C

	Imperial	Metric	American
Shortcrust pastry	8 oz	225 g	1/2 lb
Tins of corned beef	2 x 12 oz	2 x 350 g	2 x 12 oz
Onion (chopped)	6 oz	175 g	1—1 1/2 cups
Oil	1 tbsp	1 tbsp	1 tbsp
Salt and pepper			
Tabasco pepper sauce	1 tsp	1 tsp	1 tsp
Egg	1	1	1

| Cooked carrots | 4 oz | 100 g | 3/4—1 cup |
| Peas | 4 oz | 100 g | 3/4—1 cup |

Divide the pastry in half, roll out and line an 8 in/20 cm pie dish. Make up the corned beef filling by mashing up the meat in a basin. Fry the chopped onion in the oil until soft and transparent. Mix into the corned beef with the salt, pepper, Tabasco pepper sauce, egg and finally the diced carrots and the peas. When thoroughly mixed, turn on to the pastry-lined pie dish. Roll out remaining half of pastry. Dampen the pastry rim and seal on the top lid. Flute the pie edge and decorate with pastry 'leaves'. Bake at 400 °F/200 °C/Gas Mark 6 for 30 minutes.

Beef and Bacon Pie

*H or C	Imperial	Metric	American
Shortcrust pastry	12 oz	350 g	3/4 lb
Onion	1	1	1
Bacon pieces	8 oz	225 g	1/2 lb
Minced raw beef	8 oz	225 g	1/2 lb
Plain flour	1 tbsp	1 tbsp	1 tbsp
Water	1/4 pint	125 ml	5/8 cup

Pinch of fresh mixed herbs
Salt and pepper

Chop the onion and bacon in small pieces. Put them in a heavy pan and cook gently until the fat runs from the bacon and the onion becomes soft and golden. Add the minced beef and cook until it is brown. Stir in the flour, water, herbs and seasonings. Cook until the mixture is thick and well blended. Roll out the pastry into two circles and line an 8 in/20 cm pie plate. Put in the filling and cover with pastry. Bake at 400 °F/200 °C/Gas Mark 6 for 30 minutes.

Summer Lamb Pie

*H or C	Imperial	Metric	American
Puff pastry	12 oz	350 g	¾ lb
Shoulder lamb	1 lb	450 g	1 lb
Medium onion	1	1	1
Oil	1 tbsp	1 tbsp	1 tbsp
Orange	1	1	1
Stock	½ pint	250 ml	1¼ cups
Cornflour	2 tsp	2 tsp	2 tsp
Salt and pepper			
Shelled peas	4 oz	100 g	¼ lb

Roll out the pastry and use half to line a pie plate. Chop the lamb in small pieces and chop the onion finely. Fry the meat and onion in the oil until the onion is soft. Add the juice of the orange and ½ tsp grated orange rind with the stock. Simmer for 30 minutes and stir in the cornflour mixed with a little water. Stir in the peas and cool the mixture. Put into the pastry case and cover with the remaining pastry. Brush with a little beaten egg to glaze. Bake at 425 °F/220 °C/Gas Mark 7 for 40 minutes.

Chopped Pork Pie

*H or C	Imperial	Metric	American
Puff pastry	12 oz	350 g	¾ lb
Belly of pork	1 lb	450 g	1 lb
Basil	1 tsp	1 tsp	1 tsp
Salt and pepper			
Beaten egg to glaze			

Roll pastry to oblong 10 in/25 cm long. Mince or finely chop pork, mix with seasoning and with half-beaten egg. Form into 4 in/10 cm-wide roll and place down centre of pastry. Brush edges of pastry with beaten egg and fold pastry over filling. Place on a baking sheet, keeping the centre join underneath. Glaze with egg and bake at 425 °F/200 °C/Gas Mark 7 for 30 minutes.

Roman Pie

*H	Imperial	Metric	American
Shortcrust pastry	12 oz	350 g	¾ lb
Vermicelli	2 oz	50 g	2 oz
Veal or lamb	1 lb	450 g	1 lb
Cooked ham	4 oz	100 g	¼ lb
Grated lemon rind	¼ tsp	¼ tsp	¼ tsp
Salt and pepper			
Pinch of ground nutmeg			
White sauce	¼ pint	125 ml	⅝ cup
Beaten egg to glaze			

Roll out the pastry and use half to line a pie plate. Put the vermicelli into a pan of boiling salted water and boil for 5—8 minutes until tender. Drain very thoroughly. Put the vermicelli into the pastry case, pressing it round the bottom and sides so that it lines the pastry. Cut the meat into small cubes and put into the pastry case. Sprinkle on the lemon rind, salt, pepper and nutmeg. Cover with the sauce and top with remaining pastry. Brush with beaten egg to glaze. Bake at 375 °F/190 °C/Gas Mark 5 for 45 minutes.

Cheshire Pork Pie

*H or C	Imperial	Metric	American
Puff pastry	1 lb	450 g	1 lb
Loin pork	2 lb	1 kg	2 lb
Salt and pepper			
Pinch of ground nutmeg			
Eating apples	6	6	6
Sugar	2 oz	50 g	¼ cup
Dry white wine	½ pint	250 ml	1¼ cups
Butter	3 oz	75 g	⅜ cup
Beaten egg to glaze			

Roll out the pastry into two circles to fit a 10 in/25 cm pie plate. Cut the pork into thin slices and season with salt, pepper and nutmeg. Line the dish with one piece of pastry. Put in a layer of pork, then of peeled and sliced apples and sugar. Top with the remaining pork and add the wine and flakes of butter. Cover with the remaining pastry, cut a slit at the top, and brush with beaten egg. Bake at 425 °F/220 °C/Gas Mark 7 for 15 minutes, then reduce heat to 375 °F/190 °C/Gas Mark 5 and continue baking for 45 minutes.

Veal and Ham Pie

* H or C	Imperial	Metric	American
Shortcrust pastry	12 oz	350 g	¾ lb
Pie veal	1 lb	450 g	1 lb
Bacon	4 oz	100 g	¼ lb
Lemon juice	2 tsp	2 tsp	2 tsp
Pinch of thyme			
Stock or water	¼ pint	125 ml	⅝ cup
Salt and pepper			
Hard-boiled egg	1	1	1
Beaten egg to glaze			

Cut the veal into small dice and the bacon into strips. Season with lemon juice and thyme, add stock or water, and season with salt and pepper. Mix thoroughly and put into a 9 in/22.5 cm plate. Cut the hard-boiled egg into eight sections and arrange on the meat, white sides uppermost.

Cover with pastry and make a hole in the centre. Brush with beaten egg to glaze. Decorate with pastry leaves and brush them with egg. Bake at 375 °F/190 °C/ Gas Mark 5 for 30 minutes, and then at 350 °F/180 °C/Gas Mark 4 for 30 minutes.

Chicken Tarragon Pie

*H or C	Imperial	Metric	American
Shortcrust pastry	12 oz	350 g	¾ lb
Eggs	2	2	2
Milk	¼ pint	125 ml	⅝ cup
Tarragon leaves	1 tsp	1 tsp	1 tsp
Grated rind of lemon	½	½	½
Salt and pepper			
Cooked chicken meat	1 lb	450 g	1 lb

Blend together eggs and milk. Add tarragon, lemon rind, salt, pepper and chicken cut into chunky pieces. Reserve one-third of pastry. Roll out remainder into a 9 in/22.5 cm circle and use to line a 7 in/17.5 cm sandwich tin, leaving ¼ in/6 mm overlap. Fill with chicken mixture and dampen edges.

Roll out remaining pastry to an 8 in/20 cm circle and cover pie. Seal edges, trim and flute. Make six equally-spaced radial slits about 1 in/2.5 cm long from centre of pie. Dampen the centre and fold back points making a star. Bake at 425 °F/220 °C/Gas Mark 7 for 20 minutes. Reduce oven to 350 °F/180 °C/Gas Mark 4 and bake for a further 40 minutes.

Pork and Liver Pie

*H	Imperial	Metric	American
Shortcrust pastry	12 oz	350 g	¾ lb
A little milk			
Pig's liver	12 oz	350 g	¾ lb
Lean pork	1 lb	450 g	1 lb
Medium onions	2	2	2
Lard	1 oz	25 g	2 tbsp
Plain flour	2 tbsp	2 tbsp	2 tbsp
Beef stock	¼ pint	125 ml	⅝ cup
Worcestershire sauce	2 tbsp	2 tbsp	2 tbsp
Bayleaf	1	1	1
Salt and pepper			

For the filling, pour enough milk over the liver to just cover it, and leave for 30 minutes. Drain off the milk. Mince pork and liver coarsely. Gently fry the chopped onion in lard until soft, add minced pork and liver and cook, stirring, to brown. Stir in the flour, and add stock, Wocestershire sauce and bayleaf. Cover and cook gently for 30 minutes. Adjust seasoning and cool.

Divide the pastry in half. Roll out one piece and line an 8 in/20 cm pie plate. Add the cooled filling. Roll out the other pastry piece for the lid. Dampen the pastry edges on the plate, cover with the lid, seal and trim edges and flute. Roll out the pastry trimmings and cut into thin strips to make a lattice design on top. Brush with milk. Bake at 400 °F/200 °C/Gas Mark 6 for 15 minutes. Reduce oven to 350 °F/180 °C/Gas Mark 4 and bake for 30 minutes until the pastry is golden and the filling is hot.

Chicken Jalousie

*H

	Imperial	Metric	American
Puff pastry	12 oz	350 g	¾ lb
White sauce	½ pint	250 ml	1¼ cups
Cooked chicken	8 oz	225 g	½ lb
Button mushrooms	2 oz	50 g	½ cup
Salt and pepper			
Beaten egg to glaze			

Prepare the sauce and stir in diced cooked chicken and thinly sliced mushrooms. Season to taste and then set aside to cool. Roll out the pastry to a rectangle 12 x 8 in/30 x 20 cm. Cut in half across. Roll each piece of pastry to a rectangle 12 x 7 in/30 x 17.5 cm and place one half on a baking tray. Fold the other piece in half across the width. Using a sharp knife, make cuts on the folded side to within 1 in/2.5 cm of the cut edges. Open out the pastry, taking care not to stretch it. Pile the filling on to the pastry base and dampen the edges of the pastry with beaten egg; then carefully place the top in position. Flute the edges with a knife, brush the top with egg and bake at 425 °F/220 °C/ Gas Mark 7 for 40 minutes.

Curried Chicken Roll

*H or C	Imperial	Metric	American
Shortcrust pastry	8 oz	225 g	½ lb
Butter	1½ oz	40 g	3 tbsp
Cooked chicken	12 oz	350 g	¾ lb
Fresh breadcrumbs	1½ oz	40 g	½ cup
Medium onion	1	1	1
Sultanas	1 oz	25 g	¼ cup
Curry powder	2 tsp	2 tsp	2 tsp
Salt and pepper			
Egg	1	1	1
Beaten egg to glaze			

Roll out the pastry into a rectangle about 12 x 10 in/30 x 25 cm. Soften the butter and add the minced chicken, breadcrumbs, finely chopped onion and sultanas. Stir in the curry powder, salt, pepper and egg and mix well. Form into a roll about 10 in/25 cm long. Put the chicken mixture on the pastry and fold over the ends, sealing well. Put on to a baking sheet with the joint underneath. Cut three slits diagonally in the top. Brush with beaten egg to glaze. Bake at 400 °F/200 °C/Gas Mark 6 for 40 minutes.

Egg and Bacon Pie

*H or C	Imperial	Metric	American
Shortcrust pastry	12 oz	350 g	¾ lb
Streaky bacon	6 oz	150 g	6 oz
Chopped fresh parsley	1 tbsp	1 tbsp	1 tbsp
Eggs	4	4	4
Salt and pepper			

Roll out the pastry to form two rounds to fit a 7 in/17.5 cm pie plate. Line the plate with one circle of pastry. Cover the base with chopped bacon and parsley. Break in the eggs so they are equally spaced round the plate. Season well with salt and pepper. Cover carefully with remaining pastry and pinch edges together. Brush with a little milk and bake at 400 °F/200 °C/Gas Mark 6 for 30 minutes.

Kentish Bacon Pie

*H or C	Imperial	Metric	American
Puff pastry	12 oz	350 g	¾ lb
Cold boiled bacon	12 oz	350 g	¾ lb
Cherries	4 oz	100 g	¼ lb
White sauce	¼ pint	125 ml	⅝ cup
Mint jelly	1 tsp	1 tsp	1 tsp
Pepper			
Beaten egg to glaze			

Line a pie plate with two-thirds of the pastry.
Mince the bacon. Stone and quarter the cherries. Mix
together the bacon, sauce, mint jelly, pepper and cherries,
and fill the pastry case. Make a lid with the remaining
pastry. Seal the edges, make a hole in the top and brush
pastry with the beaten egg to glaze. Bake at 425 °F/220
°C/Gas Mark 7 for 15 minutes, then at 375 °F/190 °C/Gas
Mark 5 for 20 minutes until cooked through.

Bacon and Potato Pasty

*H or C	Imperial	Metric	American
Shortcrust pastry	8 oz	225 g	½ lb
Lean bacon	4 oz	100 g	¼ lb
Large onion	1	1	1
Cooked mashed potatoes	4 oz	100 g	½ cup
Grated cheese	2 oz	50 g	½ cup
Chopped parsley	1 tbsp	1 tbsp	1 tbsp
Salt and pepper			

Roll the pastry out to an 8 in/20 cm circle. Chop the
bacon and onion finely and mix with the potatoes and
cheese. Stir in the parsley, salt and pepper. Put this filling
on the pastry. Damp the edges with a little water and bring
up over the filling, pinching the edges to make a large
pasty. Bake at 375 °F/190 °C/Gas Mark 5 for 40 minutes.

Sausage Plait

*H or C	Imperial	Metric	American
Shortcrust pastry	12 oz	350 g	¾ lb
French mustard	3 tsp	3 tsp	3 tsp
Sausage meat	1 lb	450 g	1 lb
Small chopped onion	1	1	1
Mixed herbs	1 tsp	1 tsp	1 tsp
Hard-boiled eggs	2	2	2
Beaten egg to glaze			

Roll out the pastry to a 12 in/30 cm square. Spread mustard on the pastry. Mix together sausage meat, onion and herbs, and place half of this mixture down the centre third of the pastry, leaving ½ in/1.25 cm clear at top and bottom. Arrange sliced hard-boiled egg on top of sausage meat, then cover with remaining sausage meat.

Cut in from the edges to within ½ in/1.25 cm of the filling at 1 in/2.5 cm intervals on both sides of the filling. Brush edges of the pastry with beaten egg. Fold in the ½ in/1.25 cm pastry at top and bottom and fold alternate strips of pastry from the sides over the filling to form a plait, and to cover the filling. Place on a baking tray. Brush the plait with beaten egg. Bake at 400 °F/200 °C/Gas Mark 6 for 20 minutes, then reduce to 350 °F/180 °C/Gas Mark 4 and continue cooking for a further 20 minutes.

Sausage and Egg Roll

*H or C

Cheese Pastry	Imperial	Metric	American
Butter	3 oz	75 g	3/8 cup
Plain flour	6 oz	150 g	1½ cups
Pinch of salt			
Pinch of cayenne pepper			
Grated cheese	3 oz	75 g	3/4 cup
Egg yolk	1	1	1
Water to mix			
Filling			
Pork sausage meat	1 lb	450 g	1 lb
Hard-boiled eggs	4	4	4
Beaten egg to glaze			

To make pastry, rub butter into sieved flour and seasoning. Add cheese, and mix to a stiff dough with egg yolk and water. Roll to a rectangle. Flatten sausage meat on a floured board. Place sausage meat on pastry and arrange eggs in a line along centre. Fold sausage meat over eggs. Wet edges of pastry and fold over to enclose sausage meat; seal edges, using pastry scraps for decoration. Glaze with beaten egg. Bake at 400°F/200°C/Gas Mark 6 for 30 minutes, then reduce heat to 375°F/190°C/Gas Mark 5 for a further 30 minutes.

Terrine en Croute

*C	Imperial	Metric	American
Puff pastry	1 lb	450 g	1 lb
Streaky bacon rashers	1 lb	450 g	1 lb
Belly pork	1½ lb	750 g	1½ lb
Lean veal	1 lb	450 g	1 lb
Pig's liver	8 oz	225 g	½ lb
Medium onion	1	1	1
Sprig of parsley			
Pinch of ground mace			
Garlic clove	1	1	1
Few peppercorns			
Few juniper berries			
Madeira	2 fl. oz	50 ml	¼ cup
Dry white wine	¼ pint	125 ml	⅝ cup
Beaten egg to glaze			

Remove the rinds from the bacon and stretch the rashers out thinly with the back of a knife blade. Use these rashers to line a 2 pint/1 litre/5 cup terrine, setting them down on one side and across the bottom, then up the other side, leaving the ends hanging over the sides. Mince together coarsely the remaining ingredients, except egg, and then marinade in the Madeira and wine for 1 hour. Press this mixture firmly into the lined terrine then lap the ends of the bacon rashers over the top to cover completely. Put on the lid of the terrine set in a pan of hot water and bake at 350 °F/180 °C/Gas Mark 4 for 1½ hours.

Remove the terrine from the tin, uncover and leave to cool completely. Roll out the pastry to a 15 in/37.5 cm square. Trim off 1 in/2.5 cm from each side and make into pastry leaves. Set the cooled paté in the centre of the pastry, then wrap the pastry around neatly to form a closed parcel, sealing the edges with beaten egg. Set on a baking tray with the seam side underneath, brush the top with egg and decorate with pastry leaves. Bake at 425 °F/220 °C/Gas Mark 7 for 30 minutes or until a good golden colour. Set on a cooling rack and cool thoroughly before use. Serve in ½ in/1.25 cm slices for a dinner or buffet party.

Sausage and Onion Pie

*H or C	Imperial	Metric	American
Shortcrust pastry	8 oz	225 g	½ lb
Pork sausage meat	8 oz	225 g	½ lb
Medium onion	1	1	1
Egg	1	1	1
Mixed herbs	1 tbsp	1 tbsp	1 tbsp

Roll out the pastry and use half to line a pie plate. Mix the sausage meat with finely chopped onion, beaten egg and herbs. Put into the pastry case and top with the remaining pastry. Bake at 425 °F/220 °C/Gas Mark 7 for 30 minutes.

Poacher's Roll

*H or C	Imperial	Metric	American
Puff pastry	12 oz	350 g	¾ lb
Streaky bacon	6 oz	150 g	6 oz
Pork sausage meat	1 lb	450 g	1 lb
Mushrooms	2 oz	50 g	2 oz
Small onion	1	1	1
Chopped sage	½ tsp	½ tsp	½ tsp
Salt and pepper			
Beaten egg to glaze			

Roll out the pastry to an oblong 13 x 10 in/33.5 x 25 cm. Mix chopped bacon, sausage meat, chopped mushrooms, onion, sage and seasonings. Form into a sausage shape and place along the centre of the pastry. Brush the pastry edges with water and roll up, sealing the pastry at both ends to enclose the filling completely. Put the pastry roll with the join downwards on a baking sheet. Decorate the top with any pastry trimmings and make three slashes on the surface. Brush with egg and bake at 425 °F/220 °C/Gas Mark 7 for 20 minutes, then at 375 °F/190 °C/Gas Mark 5 for 40 minutes.

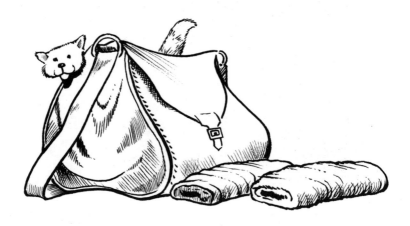

Chapter Four

FLANS

Savoury flans, or quiches as we now like to call them, should be cooked in the same way as plate pies (see previous chapter) to make the crust crisp. It is also sensible to bake the pastry 'blind', if possible, before putting in the filling, so that liquid does not sink into the crust before cooking.

A simple flan may be made with leftover meat, cheese, fish or vegetables in a white sauce or cheese sauce, but a savoury egg and cream custard makes a more attractive filling. The fillings should be thick and creamy, and well seasoned with sea salt, freshly-ground pepper, fresh herbs and spices. Gruyère cheese melts smoothly and is usually recommended for cheese flans, but grated Cheddar cheese is more economical for everyday use. Flans should not be over-garnished – some fresh parsley or other herbs, or a few tomato slices are quite enough to add colour and texture.

Shortcrust pastry is easy to handle for flans, although puff pastry may be used but this must be well-baked so that it is crisp and not too heavy and greasy, particularly if paired with a rich filling. The pastry case may be baked blind and the filling prepared well in advance of cooking. The filling should only be put into the pastry case just before baking.

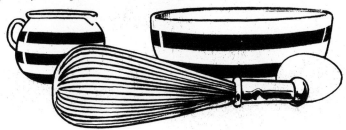

Sausage Quiche

*H or C	Imperial	Metric	American
Shortcrust pastry	12 oz	350 g	¾ lb
Butter	¾ oz	20 g	1½ tbsp
Small onion	1	1	1
Plain flour	½ oz	15 g	1 tbsp
Milk	½ pint	250 ml	1¼ cups
Single cream	¾ pint	375 ml	1½ cups
Eggs	6	6	6
Salt and pepper			
Chipolata sausages	12	12	12

Roll out the pastry to fit a 9 in/22.5 cm flan ring and bake blind at 400 °F/200 °C/Gas Mark 6 for 15 minutes. Melt the butter and toss the finely chopped onion over a gentle heat until soft but not coloured. Stir in the flour and gradually add the milk. Simmer the mixture for 15 minutes, stirring often. Cool slightly. Beat the eggs and cream together and gradually add to the onion sauce, seasoning with salt and pepper.

Grill the sausages until cooked but not brown, and drain well. Put the sausages into the pastry case like the spokes of a wheel. Pour over cream mixture. Bake at 425 °F/220 °C/Gas Mark 7 for 15 minutes. Reduce the heat to 350 °F/180 °C/Gas Mark 4 and bake for 15 minutes.

Country Sausage Flan

*H or C	Imperial	Metric	American
Shortcrust pastry	12 oz	350 g	¾ lb
Onion	1	1	1
Leeks	2	2	2
Bacon rashers	3	3	3
Mushrooms	4 oz	100 g	¼ lb
Pork sausage meat	1 lb	450 g	1 lb
Made mustard	1 tsp	1 tsp	1 tsp
Finely chopped parsley	1 tbsp	1 tbsp	1 tbsp
Salt and pepper			
Eggs	2	2	2

Line an 8 in/20 cm pie plate with the thinly rolled pastry. Chop the onion and the white part of the leeks. Take rind from the bacon and cut the rashers into strips. Wipe and chop the mushrooms. Melt a little fat in a frying pan and fry the mushrooms, onion, leeks and bacon for several minutes, until the onion is golden. Add the sausagemeat and cook for 15 minutes, stirring frequently. Add the mustard and parsley and mix well together. Season with salt and pepper and spread over the pastry case. Beat the eggs together and pour over the top. Bake at 375 °F/190 °C/Gas Mark 5 for 45 minutes.

Bacon and Egg Flan

*H or C	Imperial	Metric	American
Shortcrust pastry	8 oz	225 g	½ lb
Butter	½ oz	15 g	1 tbsp
Small onion	1	1	1
Streaky bacon	1 oz	25 g	1 oz
1 egg and 1 egg yolk			
Grated cheese .	2 oz	50 g	½ cup
Creamy milk	¼ pint	125 ml	⅝ cup
Pepper			

Roll out the pastry to line an 8 in/20 cm flan ring. Bake blind at 400 °F/200 °C/Gas Mark 6 for 10 minutes. Chop the onion finely and soften it in the butter. Add the chopped bacon and cook until the onion is golden. Remove pastry case from the oven and spread the bacon and onion mixture on the bottom. Lightly beat the egg, egg yolk, cheese, milk and a little pepper. Add salt if the bacon is not salty. Pour into the flan case and bake at 375 °F/190 °C/Gas Mark 5 for 30 minutes.

Farmhouse Flan

H or C	Imperial	Metric	American
Shortcrust pastry	12 oz	350 g	¾ lb
Minced ham	6 oz	150 g	⅓ lb
Cottage cheese	4 oz	100 g	¼ lb
Eggs	3	3	3
Soured cream	¼ pint	125 ml	⅝ cup
Salt and pepper			

Line an 8 in/20 cm pie plate with the pastry. Mix the ham and cottage cheese. Beat the eggs into the cream, mix all ingredients well and season. Pour into the pie dish and bake at 350 °F/180 °C/Gas Mark 4 for 15 minutes and at 400 °F/200 °C/Gas Mark 6 for 30 minutes until set.

Chicken Flan

H or C	Imperial	Metric	American
Shortcrust pastry	8 oz	225 g	½ lb
Small onion	1	1	1
Eating apple	1	1	1
Butter	½ oz	15 g	1 tbsp
Curry powder	1 tbsp	1 tbsp	1 tbsp
Eggs	2	2	2
Milk	¼ pint	125 ml	⅝ cup
Salt			
Cooked chicken	6 oz	150 g	6 oz

Roll out the pastry and line an 8 in/20 cm flan ring. Place the peeled and chopped onion, apple and butter into a small saucepan and cook with a lid on for 5 minutes. Add the curry powder and cook for 1 minute, and then cool. Mix together the beaten eggs, milk and salt and stir in the curry mixture. Arrange the diced chicken in the flan and pour over the egg mixture. Bake for 30 minutes at 400 °F/200 °C/Gas Mark 6.

Bacon and Mushroom Flan

*H or C	Imperial	Metric	American
Shortcrust pastry	6 oz	150 g	6 oz
Back bacon	4 oz	100 g	¼ lb
Mushrooms	4 oz	100 g	¼ lb
Butter	1 oz	25 g	2 tbsp
Large eggs	2	2	2
Milk	½ pint	300 ml	1¼ cups
Salt and pepper			
Chives or parsley			

Line a pie plate or flan ring with the pastry. Chop the bacon and mushrooms and cook in the butter until the mushrooms are just soft. Put into the pastry case. Whisk the eggs with the milk and seasoning (the bacon may be salt enough). Pour into the pastry case and bake at 425 °F/220 °C/Gas Mark 7 for 35 minutes. Scatter a few chopped chives or a little parsley on the top.

Chicken Lattice Flan

*H or C	Imperial	Metric	American
Puff pastry	8 oz	225 g	½ lb
Cooked chicken	8 oz	225 g	½ lb
Mushrooms	2 oz	50 g	2 oz
White sauce	½ pint	250 ml	1¼ cups
Salt and pepper			
Chopped parsley	1 tsp	1 tsp	1 tsp
Beaten egg to glaze			

Roll out the pastry and line a pie plate. Roll out the trimmings and cut them into ½ in/1.25 cm strips. Chop the chicken finely and slice the mushrooms thinly. Mix well with the sauce, salt, pepper and parsley. Put into the pastry case and cover with a lattice of pastry strips. Brush with beaten egg to glaze. Bake at 425 °F/220 °C/Gas Mark 7 for 40 minutes.

Corned Beef Flan

*H or C	Imperial	Metric	American
Shortcrust pastry	12 oz	350 g	¾ lb
Bacon rashers	2	2	2
Tin of corned beef	12 oz	350 g	¾ lb
Tomatoes	2	2	2
Milk	⅓ pint	175 ml	¾ cup+ 1 tbsp
Pinch of dry mustard			
Worcestershire sauce	2 tsp	2 tsp	2 tsp

Roll out pastry and line a 9 in/22.5 cm flan ring. Bake blind at 400 °F/200 °C/Gas Mark 6 for 10 minutes. Remove the rind and chop the bacon rashers. Fry until crisp. Slice the corned beef and tomatoes. Beat eggs with remaining ingredients. Remove flan from oven. Take out paper and beans. Arrange corned beef in flan and top with the bacon and tomatoes. Pour over the egg mixture and continue baking for 35 minutes until the filling is set.

Kidney Flan

*H

	Imperial	Metric	American
Shortcrust pastry	12 oz	350 g	¾ lb
Medium onion	1	1	1
Butter	1 oz	25 g	2 tbsp
Green pepper	1	1	1
Lambs' kidneys	6	6	6
Eggs	3	3	3
Milk	3 tbsp	3 tbsp	3 tbsp
Salt and pepper			

Roll out pastry and line an 8 in/20 cm flan ring. Bake blind at 400 °F/200 °C/Gas Mark 6 for 10 minutes. Fry the chopped onion in butter for 10 minutes until soft but not brown. Add chopped kidneys and green pepper. Cook gently, stirring, for 5 minutes. Remove the pan from the heat. Break eggs into a bowl, add milk, salt and pepper, and beat together with a fork. Spread the filling over the base of the flan, and pour the beaten eggs over it. Cook at 350 °F/180 °C/Gas Mark 4 for 40 minutes, until filling has set.

Chapter Five

RAISED PIES

These pies were formerly 'raised' by moulding the pastry around wooden moulds, and the pastry formed a thick wall which contained a savoury filling and could be baked without a container. It is possible to use the same technique by moulding the pastry round a jam jar, but most people now prefer to put these pies into hinged pie moulds, or cake tins with removable bases.

The pastry for raised pies is different from other pastry, as it is made with hot ingredients. The pastry has to be moulded into thick walls for strength, and also to withstand the long cooking which is necessary to penetrate the dense filling. This pastry absorbs the rich meat juices and fat so that it becomes soft inside but remains crisp outside.

Make up the hot water pastry as indicated in the first chapter: ALL ABOUT PASTRY. The pastry should be mixed well and then rested for 20 minutes before moulding or it will collapse before filling. If it is left until too cold, it will crack and be difficult to handle. If the pie is made in a tin, the sides of the tin can be removed for the last half hour of cooking so that the pastry browns well as this pastry should be richly coloured. Use about three-quarters of the pastry for the case, unless a recipe indicates otherwise, and mould it quickly with the hands up the sides of the tin, leaving no cracks. Pack the filling tightly and cover with the pastry lid, sealing the edges firmly. Glaze the pastry by brushing thickly with a beaten egg, to which a pinch of salt has been added.

One of the nicest things about a raised pie is the savoury jelly which surrounds the filling. For this, stock should be made from the bones and trimmings of the meat which is used. This needs simmering for 3—4 hours so that it will set firmly, and if a pig's trotter or calf's foot can be added, this will increase the firmness of the jelly. When the stock has simmered for 3—4 hours, strain it and reduce to about ¾ pint/375 ml/1⅞ cups stock. Season with salt and pepper and cool quickly. The stock should not be put into the pie until the pastry is cold and the filling almost firm. The stock should be just liquid enough to pour into the pie through a very small funnel (one can easily be made with a piece of foil) and the pie should be left until completely cold and firm before cutting.

Pork Pie

C	Imperial	Metric	American
Hot water pastry	1½ lb	750 g	1½ lb
Shoulder pork	2 lb	1 kg	2 lb
Chopped sage	1 tsp	1 tsp	1 tsp
Salt and pepper			
Pinch of ground nutmeg			
Jellied stock			

Make up the pastry and mould three-quarters of it. Cut the meat in small dice and mix with the sage, salt, pepper and nutmeg. Fill the case and add 3 tablespoons stock. Cover with pastry, decorate and make a hole in the top. Bake at 425 °F/220 °C/Gas Mark 7 for 30 minutes, and then at 325 °F/170 °C/Gas Mark 3 for 1½ hours, covering the pastry with greaseproof paper if it is getting too brown. Leave to cool slightly, and then pour in the stock. Leave the pie until cold and firm before cutting.

Economy Pork Pie

C	Imperial	Metric	American
Hot water pastry	1½ lb	750 g	1½ lb
Pork pieces	1 lb	450 g	1 lb
Pork sausagemeat	8 oz	225 g	½ lb
Mixed herbs	¼ tsp	¼ tsp	¼ tsp
Pinch of mace			
Bay leaf	1	1	1
Breadcrumbs	1 tbsp	1 tbsp	1 tbsp
Salt and pepper			
Hard-boiled eggs	4	4	4
Stock or water	¼ pint	125 ml	⅝ cup
Gelatine	¼ oz	8 g	1 tbsp

Make up the pastry and use three-quarters of it to mould the case. Chop or mince the pork and mix with the sausagemeat, herbs and spices and breadcrumbs. Season well with salt and pepper. Put half the mixture into the pie case and arrange the hard-boiled eggs on top. Fill up with remaining mixture and 1 tbsp stock or water. Cover with a pastry lid and decorate. Bake at 425 °F/220 °C/Gas Mark 7 for 30 minutes and then at 325 °F/170 °C/Gas Mark 3 for 1½ hours. Cool slightly and pour in stock with gelatine dissolved in it. Leave until cold and firm before cutting.

Pork and Apple Pies

C	Imperial	Metric	American
Hot water pastry	1½ lb	750 g	1½ lb
Lean pork	1 lb	450 g	1 lb
Large onion	1	1	1
Cooking apple	1	1	1
White wine or cider	2 tbsp	2 tbsp	2 tbsp
Salt and pepper			
Beaten egg to glaze			
Stock or water	½ pint	250 ml	1¼ cups
Gelatine	1 tsp	1 tsp	1 tsp

Mix together the minced meat and onion, chop the apple and soak in the wine for 10 minutes. Add to the meat and onion, together with salt and pepper. Divide the pastry into eight pieces. For each piece proceed as follows: Cut off one-third of the pastry for the lids and put aside. Roll out the remaining pastry to a round approximately 5½ in/13 cm diameter. Dredge a 2½ in/6 cm upturned jar or canister heavily with flour. Lift the pastry on a rolling pin and transfer it to the mould. Shape the pastry by pressing it firmly against the sides of the mould. Cut a piece of greaseproof paper or baking parchment long enough to go completely round the pie. Wrap the paper round the pastry; secure with string or a pin. Allow pastry to rest in a cool place until firm. Turn the mould over and ease it out of the pastry case, twisting at first to loosen it. Repeat to make eight pies.

Fill the pie cases with the meat mixture, packing it well at the sides to hold the shape of the pies. Roll out each lid to the top of the pie, brush the edge of each lid with beaten egg and press this to the upper edge of the pie between finger and thumb. Hold the edges between finger and thumb to knock them up and flute them. Glaze the tops with beaten egg, using any remaining pastry for decoration. Make holes to let out the steam.

Bake at 400 °F/200 °C/Gas Mark 6 for 30 minutes. Remove paper from the sides, cook for a further 30 minutes reducing the heat to 350 °F/180 °C/Gas Mark 4. Allow to cool. Make the jelly by placing the stock and gelatine in a saucepan. Stir on a low heat until the gelatine has dissolved; season to taste. Pour the cooled jelly into the pies. Allow to set before serving.

Veal and Ham Pie

C	Imperial	Metric	American
Hot water pastry	1 lb	450 g	1 lb
Pie veal	1 lb	450 g	1 lb
Raw ham or lean bacon	4 oz	100 g	¼ lb
Pinch of thyme			
Salt and pepper			
Hard-boiled egg	1	1	1
Jellied stock	½ pint	250 ml	1¼ cups

Mould three-quarters of the pastry. Cut the veal and ham into small pieces and mix with the thyme, salt and pepper. Put half the mixture into the pie case and put the egg in the centre. Cover with the remaining meat mixture and add 2 tbsp stock. Cover with pastry and decorate. Bake at 425 °F/220 °C/Gas Mark 7 for 30 minutes, and then at 325 °F/170 °C/Gas Mark 3 for 1½ hours, covering the pastry with paper if it browns too quickly. Cool slightly and pour in the stock. Leave until cold before cutting.

Game Pie

	Imperial	Metric	American
C			
Hot water pastry	1½ lb	750 g	1½ lb
Pork sausagemeat	12 oz	350 g	¾ lb
Lean bacon or uncooked ham	4 oz	100 g	¼ lb
Lean chuck steak	6 oz	150 g	6 oz
Pheasant	1	1	1
Salt and pepper			
Jellied stock	¼—½ pint	125—250 ml	⅝—1¼ cups

Instead of the pheasant, grouse, partridge or pigeons may be used. If venison is available, this can be used instead of the chuck steak. Pieces of hare and/or rabbit may also be included. A total of about 1¼ lb/550 g/1¼ lb mixed meat and game is needed in addition to the sausagemeat and bacon. The pie looks most attractive if made in an oval hinged game-pie mould, but a round cake tin can be used instead.

Make up the pastry and use three-quarters of it to line the mould, pressing the pastry well into the sides of the tin. Line the pastry with a thin layer of sausagemeat. Cut the bacon and steak into small cubes. Strip the flesh from the game bird or animal and cut it in small pieces. Mix the meats well together and season with salt and pepper. Add about 4 tbsp stock and pack the meat into the case.

Cover with remaining pastry and decorate, and make a hole in the centre. Bake at 425 °F/220 °C/Gas Mark 7 for 30 minutes; then lower heat to 375 °F/190 °C/Gas Mark 5 for 30 minutes. Reduce heat again to 350 °F/180 °C/Gas Mark 4 and bake for 30 minutes more. Cover the pie with greaseproof paper if it is becoming too brown. Take the pie from the oven, fill up with hot stock and leave to cool. Do not take from the tin until the pie is completely cold and the stock is set.

A game bird for a pie need not be plucked. Just loosen the skin at the neck, make a cut along the backbone, and skin the bird, removing the feathers at the same time.

Hare Pie

C	Imperial	Metric	American
Hot water pastry	1 lb	450 g	1 lb
Joints of hare	3	3	3
Fresh herbs	1 tsp	1 tsp	1 tsp
Salt and pepper			
Red wine or cider	3 tbsp	3 tbsp	3 tbsp
Cold jellied stock			
Beaten egg to glaze			

Chop or mince the hare finely, season with herbs, salt and pepper, and leave to stand overnight in wine or cider. Make up the pastry and line a 7 in/17.5 cm cake tin with removable bottom. Mix the hare with a tablespoon of stock and put into the pastry case. Brush the top edge with beaten egg, and put on the lid. Glaze the lid with beaten egg and make a hole in the centre.

Bake at 400 °F/200 °C/Gas Mark 6 for 20 minutes; then reduce heat to 350 °F/180 °C/Gas Mark 4 for one hour, covering the pastry to prevent burning. Cool the pie and pour in a little cold jellied stock which is almost at setting point. Leave in tin until completely cold.

Chicken and Bacon Raised Pie

C	Imperial	Metric	American
Hot water pastry	1½ lb	750 g	1½ lb
Collar bacon	10 oz	300 g	10 oz
Fresh chicken	10 oz	300 g	10 oz
Chopped parsley	1 tbsp	1 tbsp	1 tbsp
Grated rind of small lemon	1	1	1
Salt and pepper			
A little stock or water			
Hard-boiled egg	1	1	1
Beaten egg to glaze			
Gelatine	2 tsp	2 tsp	2 tsp
Chicken stock	½ pint	250 ml	1¼ cups

Mix together diced bacon, diced chicken, parsley, lemon rind, salt and pepper. Moisten with a little stock or water. Knead the pastry for 2 minutes until smooth and free from cracks. Roll out two-thirds of the pastry, keeping reserved pastry under a bowl in a warm place. Use pastry to line a 6 in/15 cm loose-based round cake tin. Half fill the pastry case with the meat mixture. Put the egg in the centre and add the remaining meat mixture. Roll out remaining pastry, cover and decorate pie with pastry trimmings. Glaze the top with a little beaten egg.

Bake in the centre of oven at 425 °F/220 °C/Gas Mark 7 for 15—20 minutes. Then reduce the heat to 350 °F/180 °C/Gas Mark 4 and continue cooking for a further 1—1½ hours, or until meat feels tender when tested with a skewer. When cold, fill the pie up with jelly stock made by dissolving the gelatine in chicken stock. Allow to set in the tin.

Chapter Six

INDIVIDUAL PIES

Small pies and pastry items are always popular because they can be used as snacks and packed meals, or make a main meal with vegetables or salad; they can also be used for parties. Pastry makes the most of a small quantity of ingredients, so that a few ounces of meat can be extended to serve many people with pasties or little pies. If these are to be packed in a lunch box or packed in any way, shortcrust pastry will provide a firmer casing for the filling; for parties or for meals at home, a lighter puff pastry may be preferred.

Devon Lamb Pies

* H or C	Imperial	Metric	American
Puff pastry	12 oz	350 g	¾ lb
Cold cooked lamb	8 oz	225 g	½ lb
Cold boiled ham or bacon	2 oz	50 g	2 oz
Plain flour	1 tsp	1 tsp	1 tsp
Chopped parsley	1 tsp	1 tsp	1 tsp
Mixed fresh herbs	½ tsp	½ tsp	½ tsp
Salt and pepper			
Thick brown gravy	¼ pint	125 ml	⅝ cup

Chop the lamb and ham or bacon. Mix with the flour, parsley and herbs. Season to taste. Roll out the pastry and cut out twelve rounds. Line six individual patty tins and fill these with the meat mixture. Add gravy to each, put on lids and make a slit in the centre of each. Bake at 400 °F/200 °C/Gas Mark 6 for 30 minutes. Heat any left-over gravy and pour it into the pies before serving.

Lamb Parcels

H	Imperial	Metric	American
Puff pastry	8 oz	225 g	½ lb
Lamb cutlets	4	4	4
Eating apples	2	2	2
Squeeze of lemon juice			
Salt and pepper			
Pinch of curry powder			
Beaten egg to glaze			

Roll the pastry into a square and cut into four triangles. Season the cutlets with salt, pepper and lemon juice, rubbing the seasoning well in. Peel and slice the apples and toss them in lemon juice. Put one lamb cutlet on each triangle of pastry and top with apple slices. Damp the edges of the pastry and form into parcels, leaving the cutlet bones sticking out. Brush the pastry with beaten egg to glaze. Put a twist of foil round each cutlet bone so that they will not colour as the pastry cooks. Bake at 425 °F/ 220°C/Gas Mark 5 for 35 minutes.

Cornish Pasties

*H or C	Imperial	Metric	American
Shortcrust pastry	2 lb	1 kg	2 lb
Chuck or blade steak	8 oz	225 g	½ lb
Small onion	1	1	1
Small turnip	1	1	1
Small carrot	1	1	1
Medium potato	1	1	1
Salt and pepper			
Beaten egg to glaze			

Cut meat into small pieces. Peel vegetables and cut into ¼ in/6 mm dice. Add to meat and mix well. Season well with salt and pepper. Roll pastry out thinly. Using a small saucepan lid or plate as a guide, cut out twenty-four 5 in/12.5 cm circles of pastry. Divide filling between pastry rounds, damp edges of pastry, and draw edges together to form a join across the top. Press well together and flute edges. Place on a baking tray, brush with beaten egg and bake at 400 °F/200 °C/Gas Mark 6 for 15 minutes. Reduce heat to 350 °F/180 °C/Gas Mark 4 and cook for 35 minutes, until the pastry is golden and filling tender.

Beef Patties

* H or C

Pastry	Imperial	Metric	American
Plain flour	1 lb	450 g	1 lb
Lard or dripping	6 oz	150 g	¾ cup
Water	¼ pint	125 ml	⅝ cup
Filling			
Beef	6 oz	150 g	6 oz
Medium onion	1	1	1
Thick brown gravy	2 tbsp	2 tbsp	2 tbsp
Salt and pepper			

Make the pastry, cut into rounds, and line some patty tins. Cut the meat into small pieces, or mince finely with the onion; mix with the gravy, onion and seasoning. Place a spoonful in each pastry case, put on pastry lids and press the edges together. Bake at 375 °F/190 °C/Gas Mark 5 for 30 minutes.

Samosas

H
Pastry

	Imperial	Metric	American
Self-raising flour or flour sifted with 1½ tsp baking powder	6 oz	150 g	1½ cups
Shredded suet	3 oz	75 g	⅜ cup
Pinch of salt			

Filling

Cooked lamb	6 oz	150 g	6 oz
Small onion	1	1	1
Curry powder	1 tsp	1 tsp	1 tsp
Oil	1 tbsp	1 tbsp	1 tbsp
Salt and pepper			
Sweet chutney	1 tbsp	1 tbsp	1 tbsp
Deep oil for frying			

Make up pastry by mixing the flour, suet and salt with enough cold water to make a firm dough. Roll out and cut into eight rounds. Chop the lamb finely. Grate the onion and mix with the curry powder. Fry in the oil for 5 minutes. Add the lamb and continue cooking for 5 minutes more. Season with salt, pepper and chutney and cool. Put a spoonful of the mixture in the centre of each pastry round. Bring up edges and pinch together to make a pasty shape. Fry in hot oil for about 5 minutes until the pastry is golden. Serve with chutney.

Spiced Beef Puffs

*H or C	Imperial	Metric	American
Puff pastry	1½ lb	750 g	1½ lb
Oil	1 tbsp	1 tbsp	1 tbsp
Butter	½ oz	15 g	1 tbsp
Medium onion	1	1	1
Raw minced beef	8 oz	225 g	½ lb
Small green pepper	1	1	1
Ground ginger	¼ tsp	¼ tsp	¼ tsp
Chili powder	¼ tsp	¼ tsp	¼ tsp
Tomato puree	1 tbsp	1 tbsp	1 tbsp
Salt and pepper			
Stuffed olives	6	6	6

1 egg, beaten with 1 tbsp water

Heat oil and butter in a pan and fry chopped onion gently until soft. Stir in mince and cook until brown, stirring all the time. Add chopped green pepper, ginger, chili powder, tomato puree and salt and pepper. Cover and cook gently for 10 minutes. Add stuffed olives and allow mixture to cool. Roll out pastry and cut into eight 6 in/15 cm circles and prick with a fork. Place a tablespoon of beef mixture in centre of each and dampen edges. Fold in half and seal edges firmly. Chill for 30 minutes. Brush tops with egg glaze and bake at 425 °F/220 °C/Gas Mark 7 for 20 minutes until risen and golden.

Fried Meat Pies

H	Imperial	Metric	American
Shortcrust pastry	12 oz	350 g	¾ lb
Medium onion	1	1	1
Lard	1 tbsp	1 tbsp	1 tbsp
Minced raw beef	1 lb	450 g	1 lb
Stock	½ pint	250 ml	1¼ cups
Chopped parsley	2 tsp	2 tsp	2 tsp
Salt and pepper			
Flour	2 tbsp	2 tbsp	2 tbsp
Chopped hard-boiled eggs	2	2	2
Hot deep fat for frying			

Roll out the pastry thinly and cut into six circles the size of a saucer. Chop the onion finely and soften it in the lard. Add the beef, stock, parsley, salt and pepper to taste, and simmer, with a lid on, for 30 minutes. Blend the flour with a little cold water and stir into the mixture. Add the eggs and leave to cool. Put meat mixture on one side of each circle, fold over pastry to form a turnover, and pinch the edges to seal them.

Fry in hot deep fat for about 3 minutes until golden. The filling can be varied by using corned beef flavoured with a little tomato purée; a little chopped green pepper can be added to the basic mixture. These are delicious eaten very hot with a crisp salad.

Little Chicken Pies

H	Imperial	Metric	American
Puff pastry	12 oz	350 g	¾ lb
Small chicken	1	1	1
Mushrooms	4 oz	100 g	¼ lb
Hard-boiled egg yolks	4	4	4
Medium onion	1	1	1
Vinegar	1 tbsp	1 tbsp	1 tbsp
Chopped parsley	1 tsp	1 tsp	1 tsp
Salt	½ tsp	½ tsp	½ tsp
Worcestershire sauce	½ tsp	½ tsp	½ tsp
Streaky bacon	4 rashers	4 rashers	4 rashers

Stock made from chicken carcass

Take the flesh in neat pieces from an uncooked chicken, and simmer the carcass in water for an hour to make stock. Mix together pieces of light and dark flesh, sliced mushrooms, chopped egg yolks, finely chopped onion, vinegar, parsley, salt, sauce and chopped bacon. Put into four individual pie dishes. Half-fill each dish with stock and cover with pastry. Brush the pastry with a little beaten egg, make an air vent in each, and bake at 350 °F/180 °C/Gas Mark 4 for 1 hour.

Sausage Pasties

H or C	Imperial	Metric	American
Puff pastry	8 oz	225 g	1/2 lb
Sausage meat	8 oz	225 g	1/2 lb
Dried sage	1/4 tsp	1/4 tsp	1/4 tsp
Hard-boiled eggs	2	2	2
Small onion	1	1	1
Salt and pepper			
Beaten egg to glaze			

Mix sausage meat, sage, eggs, grated onion and seasonings together. Roll out pastry thinly and cut into four 6 in/15 cm circles. Divide filling between pastry rounds, leaving a clear edge all round. Dampen the edges. Fold one side of pastry over the filling, and seal edges firmly. Place on a baking sheet. Brush with beaten egg and make two neat slits in the top of each one with a sharp knife and bake at 425 °F/220 °C/Gas Mark 7 for 20 minutes, or until browned. Reduce heat to 350 °F/180 °C/Gas Mark 4 and cook for a further 5 minutes.

Country Sausage Rolls

*H or C	Imperial	Metric	American
Bran cereal	1 oz	25 g	1/2 cup
Milk	4 tbsp	4 tbsp	4 tbsp
Self-raising flour or flour sifted with 1 tsp baking powder	5 oz	125 g	1 1/4 cups
Salt and pepper			
Butter	1 1/2 oz	40 g	3 tbsp
Grated cheese	1 oz	25 g	1/8 cup
Made mustard	1 tsp	1 tsp	1 tsp
Chipolata sausages	8 oz	225 g	1/2 lb

Put the bran into a bowl with the milk and leave to soak for 10 minutes. Sieve the flour, salt and pepper and rub in the butter. Stir in the cheese and soaked bran and knead well. Roll into a square. Spread the pastry with mustard and cut into ½ in/1.25 cm strips. Twist a strip of pastry round each sausage, overlapping the edges. If necessary, join two pieces of pastry so that the sausages are covered. Put on a greased baking sheet and bake at 425 °F/ 220 °C/Gas Mark 7 for 15 minutes.

Special Sausage Rolls

* H or C	Imperial	Metric	American
Puff pastry	1 lb	450 g	1 lb
Large pork sausages	8	8	8
Rashers of streaky bacon	8	8	8
Mango chutney			
Beaten egg for glaze			

Cut pastry in two and roll each piece to a strip 16 x 16 in/40 x 40 cm approximately. Skin the sausages and shape neatly with floured hands. Stretch the bacon rashers with the flat blade of a knife and spread with chutney. Wrap each sausage in a rasher of bacon. Place four sausages on each strip of pastry, brush the edge with beaten egg. Fold over the pastry, seal the edge well and knock up with the back of a knife. Cut each piece into four sausage rolls. Place on a baking tray and brush with beaten egg. Bake at 425 °F/220 °C/Gas Mark 7 for 25 minutes.

Curried Ham Turnovers

*H or C	Imperial	Metric	American
Shortcrust pastry	1 lb	450 g	1 lb
Cooked ham	6 oz	150 g	6 oz
Soured cream	3 tbsp	3 tbsp	3 tbsp
Mayonnaise	2 tbsp	2 tbsp	2 tbsp
Pinch of salt			
Dry mustard	¼ tsp	¼ tsp	¼ tsp
Shake of Cayenne pepper			
Curry powder	1 tsp	1 tsp	1 tsp
Chopped chives	2 tbsp	2 tbsp	2 tbsp
Egg yolk	1	1	1

Roll out the pastry ¼ in/6 mm thick and cut into eighteen 3 in/7.5 cm rounds. Mince the ham or chop it finely, and mix in a bowl with cream, mayonnaise, seasonings and chives. Put 1 heaped tsp of the mixture on one side of each pastry round. Moisten the edges of each round with water and fold over. Press the edges together firmly and prick the top of the turnovers with the tip of a sharp knife. Brush the pastry with the egg yolk mixed with 3 tsp of water. Put on to baking sheets and bake at 425 °F/ 220 °C/Gas Mark 7 for 15 minutes until golden.

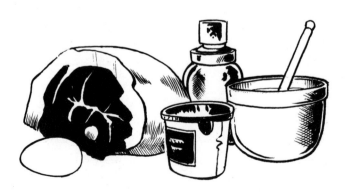

Bacon & Sweetcorn Pies

*H or C	Imperial	Metric	American
Shortcrust pastry	1½ lb	750 g	1½ lb
Rashers of streaky bacon	4	4	4
Butter	½ oz	15 g	1 tbsp
Medium onion	1	1	1
Cooked ham	6 oz	15 g	6 oz
Sweetcorn kernels	6 oz	150 g	1¼ cups
Made mustard	½ tsp	½ tsp	½ tsp
Salt and pepper			
Tomatoes	3	3	3

1 egg, beaten with 1 tbsp water

Fry bacon in pan without fat until crisp, then remove. Add butter to pan and cook onion gently until soft. Remove ham from bone and shop. Mix all filling ingredients together except tomatoes. Cut off one-third of pastry and keep for lids. Roll out remaining two-thirds and cut into twelve 4 in/10 cm circles. Use to line deep foil baking cases about 3 in/7.5 cm across. Half-fill with ham mixture, add tomato slices and cover with remaining filling. Roll out remaining pastry and cut into circles for lids. Dampen edges of pies, cover with lids and seal well. Make a small hole in centre of each pie. Brush with egg glaze. Bake at 375 °F/190 °C/Gas Mark 5 for 45 minutes until pastry is golden brown.

Kidney and Bacon Pasties

*H or C

	Imperial	Metric	American
Shortcrust pastry	1 lb	450 g	1 lb
Minced raw steak	8 oz	225 g	½ lb
Streaky bacon	6 oz	150 g	6 oz
Lambs' kidneys	4 oz	100 g	¼ lb
Large onion	1	1	1
Salt and pepper			
Worcestershire sauce	½ tsp	½ tsp	½ tsp

Roll out the pastry and cut it into six 7 in/17.5 cm rounds. Chop the bacon, kidney and onion, and mix with the steak, seasoning and sauce. Put the mixture on to half of each round and fold over pastry. Pinch the edges together and brush with a little beaten egg. Bake at 425°F/220 °C/Gas Mark 7 for 15 minutes, and then at 350°F/180 °C/Gas Mark 4 for 45 minutes.

Luncheon Squares

* H or C

	Imperial	Metric	American
Shortcrust pastry	12 oz	350 g	¾ lb
Canned luncheon meat	8 oz	225 g	½ lb
Medium onion	1	1	1
Medium potato	1	1	1
Lard	1 oz	25 g	2 tbsp
White sauce	¼ pint	125 ml	⅝ cup
Chopped parsley	1 tsp	1 tsp	1 tsp
Grated lemon rind	1 tsp	1 tsp	1 tsp
Salt and pepper			

Roll out the pastry and use half to line an 8 in/ 20 cm square tin. Cut the meat into small cubes. Chop the onion and potato finely and cook in the hot lard until just soft. Drain off surplus fat. Mix the onion and potato with the meat, sauce, parsley, lemon rind, salt and pepper. Put into the pastry case and cover with the remaining pastry. Bake at 425 °F/220 °C/Gas Mark 7 for 15 minutes, then at 350 °F/180 °C/Gas Mark 4 for 15 minutes. Cut into nine squares to serve.

Pork Pasties

*H or C	Imperial	Metric	American
Shortcrust pastry	1 lb	450 g	1 lb
Hard-boiled eggs	2	2	2
Cold pork	8 oz	225 g	½ lb
Eating apples	3	3	3
Spring onions	6	6	6
Sage			
Salt and pepper			
Beaten egg to glaze			

Roll out the pastry and cut into four large circles using a saucer. Mix together chopped eggs, chopped pork, apples and onions. Season with sage, salt and pepper. Divide mixture between the four pastry circles, brush with egg, and bring the edges to meet on the tops of the pasties. Place on a baking sheet and brush with egg. Bake at 400 °F/200 °C/Gas Mark 6 for 30 minutes.

Turkey Tartlets

H or C	Imperial	Metric	American
Shortcrust pastry	12 oz	350 g	¾ lb
Onion	1	1	1
Butter	1 oz	25 g	2 tbsp
Tin of apricot halves	15 oz	425 g	15 oz
Curry paste	2 tsp	2 tsp	2 tsp
Lemon juice	2 tsp	2 tsp	2 tsp
Soured cream	¼ pint	125 ml	⅝ cup
Cooked turkey, chopped	10 oz	300 g	10 oz
Tabasco sauce	½ tsp	½ tsp	½ tsp
Salt and pepper			
Cooked peas	4 oz	100 g	¼ lb
Beaten egg to glaze			

Cook the chopped onion in butter until golden. Add the apricot halves. Simmer 20 minutes until reduced to a thick pulp. Thin the curry paste with a little water and add to the apricots with lemon juice. Stir in the soured cream and chopped turkey pieces. Bring to the boil and simmer gently for 10 minutes. Add the Tabasco sauce and season to taste. Remove from heat and stir in the peas. Leave covered to cool.

Halve the pastry and roll out one half. Cut out 5 in/ 12.5 cm rounds to line large individual patty tins. Divide the cooled turkey filling equally between the tarts. Using the remaining pastry, cut out and cover the tarts, glazing with beaten egg to make the edges stick. Pinch the edges together with thumb and forefinger and decorate tops with pastry 'leaves'. Glaze with beaten egg. Cook at 425 °F/ 220 °C/Gas Mark 7 for 20 minutes.

Chapter Seven

SAVOURY PUDDINGS

Suet pastry is an old-fashioned favourite used for extending savoury fillings. It may be used as a complete casing for the filling in a basin, or just as a top crust; an alternative is to roll the pastry round a dry filling, rather like a Swiss roll.

To make a suet crust (if you want to make up your own recipes) allow 1 oz/25 g flour/¼ cup to ½ oz/15 g/ 1 tbsp shredded suet for one helping of pudding. For a family-sized (4—5 person) pudding, allow 8 oz/225 g/ 2 cups flour to 4 oz/100 g/½ cup suet, which will allow for some second helpings. For whatever sized pudding you need, always allow half as much suet as flour, and use either self-raising flour, or plain flour with baking powder. Always add a pinch of salt and just enough cold water to give a soft but firm crust which can be rolled out

To cover a pudding, use kitchen foil or double greaseproof paper brushed with melted fat, or a pudding cloth. When wrapping roly-poly puddings, greaseproof paper covered with foil will be satisfactory, or a lightly floured pudding cloth. Tie the ends of the pudding with string, allowing room for expansion. When covering a pudding in a basin, put a pleat in the covering so the top crust can expand. Put the pudding into a pan of boiling water to come about halfway up the basin, or immerse a long pudding. Cover and keep the pan on medium heat so that the water bubbles gently. Top up the water about every 30 minutes, and always use boiling water for this purpose.

Steak and Kidney Pudding

*H	Imperial	Metric	American
Self-raising flour or flour sifted with 2 tsp baking powder	8 oz	225 g	2 cups
Shredded suet	4 oz	100 g	½ cup
Salt and pepper			
Water	6 tbsp	6 tbsp	6 tbsp
Stewing steak	1 lb	450 g	1 lb
Lambs' kidneys	3	3	3
or			
Ox kidney	4 oz	100 g	¼ lb

Cut steak into thin pieces and chop kidney in small pieces. If liked, wrap a piece of meat round each piece of kidney, but otherwise just mix the two meats. Mix flour, suet, salt and pepper to a firm paste with water. Line a greased basin with two-thirds of the pastry. Put in the meat, and season well with salt and pepper and add a sprinkling of flour. Add water or stock almost to the top of the basin. Cover with remaining pastry and seal edges. Cover and steam for 4 hours.

Variations: Either add 1 small chopped onion or substitute 3 sliced onions for kidney. 2 oz/50 g/½ cup chopped mushrooms may be added.

Bacon Roll

H	Imperial	Metric	American
Self-raising flour or flour sifted with 2 tsp baking powder	8 oz	225 g	2 cups
Shredded suet	3 oz	75 g	⅜ cup
Salt and pepper			
Chopped mixed bacon and onion	6 oz	150 g	¾ cup

Make suet pastry, using just enough water to make a firm dough. Roll into a rectangle and put on bacon and onion, and plenty of seasoning. A little chopped sage may be added. Roll up like a Swiss roll in a floured cloth and boil for 1½ hours. Serve with gravy.

Chicken Pudding

*H	Imperial	Metric	American
Self-raising flour or flour sifted with 3 tsp baking powder	12 oz	350 g	3 cups
Shredded suet	6 oz	150 g	¾ cup
Pinch of salt			
Chicken	4 lb	2 kg	4 lb
Medium onion	1	1	1
Garlic clove	1	1	1
Bayleaf			
Salt and pepper			
Chopped parsley	2 tsp	2 tsp	2 tsp

Make up suet pastry with enough water to give a firm dough. Line a large basin with two-thirds of the pastry. Skin the chicken and cut flesh from the wings, legs and breast and cut into small pieces. Put the bones and skin into water to cover and simmer to make stock. Put alternate layers of chicken, chopped onion and garlic into the basin, tucking the bayleaf in the centre. Season layers with salt, pepper and parsley. Cover with ½ pint/300 ml/ 1¼ cups chicken stock. Cover with remaining pastry. Cover and steam for 4 hours. Serve with more chicken stock, or with parsley sauce.

Mince Layer Pudding

*H	Imperial	Metric	American
Self-raising flour or flour sifted with 2 tsp baking powder	8 oz	225 g	2 cups
Shredded suet	4 oz	100 g	¼ lb
Pinch of salt			
Cooked minced beef	1 lb	450 g	1 lb
Medium onion	1	1	1
Salt and pepper			

Prepare the suet pastry with flour, suet, salt and water, and roll out. Line a basin with half the pastry. The meat may be left from a joint, or fresh mince may be used after simmering in a little stock or gravy. Mix meat with the chopped onion and seasoning. Put a layer of this mixture at the bottom of the basin, and then a thin layer of suet pastry. Continue in layers until the basin is full, ending with a pastry layer. Cover and steam for 2 hours. Serve with parsley sauce or gravy.

Rabbit Pudding

*H	Imperial	Metric	American
Self-raising flour or flour sifted with 2 tsp baking powder	8 oz	225 g	2 cups
Shredded suet	4 oz	100 g	½ cup
Salt and pepper			
Water	6 tbsp	6 tbsp	6 tbsp
Small rabbit	1	1	1
Sage	½ tsp	½ tsp	½ tsp
Sliced onions	2	2	2
Sliced tomatoes	2	2	2
Chopped mushrooms	2 oz	50 g	2 oz

Make pastry in the same way as for steak and kidney pudding. Fill pudding with rabbit joints, water, sage, onions, tomatoes and mushrooms tucked into the corners around the joints. Cover and steam for 4 hours.

Pigeon Pudding

*H	Imperial	Metric	American
Self-raising flour or flour sifted with 2 tsp baking powder	8 oz	225 g	2 cups
Shredded suet	4 oz	100 g	½ cup
Pinch of salt			
Pigeons	2	2	2
Shin beef	8 oz	225 g	½ lb
Lamb's kidney	1	1	1
Salt and pepper			
Beef stock	½ pint	300 ml	1¼ cups

Make up the suet pastry and line a basin with two-thirds of the dough. Skin the pigeons, and cut off the breasts with a sharp pointed knife. Cut the beef in small cubes and chop the kidney. Arrange in layers in the basin, seasoning well. Pour in the stock and cover with the remaining pastry. Cover and steam for 2½ hours.

Pork and Sausage Pudding

*H

	Imperial	Metric	American
Self-raising flour or flour sifted with 2 tsp baking powder	8 oz	225 g	2 cups
Shredded suet	4 oz	100 g	½ cup
Pinch of salt			
Lean pork	1½ lb	750 g	1½ lb
Sausage meat	12 oz	350 g	¾ lb
Sage leaves	6	6	6
Medium onion	1	1	1
Salt and pepper			

Make suet pastry with the flour, suet, salt and enough water to make a stiff paste. Roll out and line a basin with two-thirds of the pastry. Cut the pork in small thin slices and put into the lined basin. Add the sausage meat, sage, finely chopped onion, salt and pepper. Cover with the remaining pastry. Cover and boil for 4 hours.

Pork and Apple Pudding

*H

	Imperial	Metric	American
Self-raising flour or flour sifted with 2 tsp baking powder	8 oz	225 g	2 cups
Shredded suet	4 oz	100 g	½ cup
Fresh lean pork	8 oz	225 g	½ lb
Medium cooking apple	1	1	1
Salt and pepper			
Sage			
Stock or water			

Prepare pastry with flour and suet and enough water to make a firm paste. Line basin with pastry, and put in pork (cut in squares), chopped apple, salt and pepper, a good pinch of chopped sage and stock to cover. Put on pastry lid, cover and boil for 4 hours.

Bacon Layer Pudding

H	Imperial	Metric	American
Self-raising flour or flour sifted with 1½ tsp baking powder	6 oz	150 g	1½ cups
Shredded suet	3 oz	75 g	3 oz
Pinch of salt			
Bacon	8 oz	225 g	½ lb
Medium onions	2	2	2
Medium carrots	2	2	2

Make up suet pastry with enough water to make a firm dough. Roll out thinly and cut a round to fit the bottom of a greased 2 pint/1 litre/5 cup pudding basin. Chop the bacon. Grate the onions and carrots together. Put a layer of bacon on the pastry and top with a little onion and carrot. Top with another layer of pastry. Continue these layers until the basin is full, topping with pastry. Cover and steam for 2 hours. Serve with gravy.

Kidney Pudding

*H	Imperial	Metric	American
Sheeps' kidneys	3	3	3
Shredded suet	1 tsp	1 tsp	1 tsp
Breadcrumbs	3 oz	75 g	3/4 cup
Chopped parsley	2 tsp	2 tsp	2 tsp
Mixed herbs	1 tsp	1 tsp	1 tsp
Pinch of ground nutmeg			
Salt and pepper			
Egg	1	1	1
Milk	3 fl. oz	75 ml	3/8 cup

Skin the kidneys and mince them or chop them very finely. Mix with the suet and the breadcrumbs. Add the parsley, herbs, salt and pepper. Mix the egg and milk and stir into the breadcrumb mixture. Put into a greased pudding basin, cover and steam for 1½ hours. Serve with rich gravy.

Liver Dumpling

H	Imperial	Metric	American
Self-raising flour or flour sifted with 3 tsp baking powder	12 oz	350 g	3 cups
Shredded suet	6 oz	150 g	3/4 cup
Liver	8 oz	225 g	1/2 lb
Streaky bacon	8 oz	225 g	1/2 lb
Large onions	2	2	2
Chopped sage	2 tsp	2 tsp	2 tsp
Salt and pepper			

Mix the flour and suet to a firm dough with cold water and a pinch of salt. Roll out to a rectangle. Chop the liver and bacon very small. Spread over the suet pastry. Grate the onions on top and cover with sage, salt and pepper. Roll up tightly like a Swiss roll and tie in a floured cloth. Boil for 2½ hours. Serve with gravy.

Kidney Dumpling

H	Imperial	Metric	American
Self-raising flour or flour sifted with 2 tsp baking powder	8 oz	225 g	2 cups
Shredded suet	4 oz	100 g	½ cup
Pinch of salt			
Lamb's kidneys	4	4	4
Large onions	4	4	4
Salt and pepper			

Make up suet pastry with the flour, suet, salt and enough water to make a firm paste. Roll out in a square and cut four 6 in/15 cm squares. Skin the kidneys and remove cores. Peel the onions and scoop out the centres. Season inside the cavities and put a kidney in each one. Put an onion on to each pastry and pinch up the corners to enclose the onions completely. Turn upside down on a baking sheet so that the joins come underneath. Bake at 350 °F/180 °C/Gas Mark 4 for 1¼ hours. Lift carefully off the baking sheet and serve with gravy.

INDEX